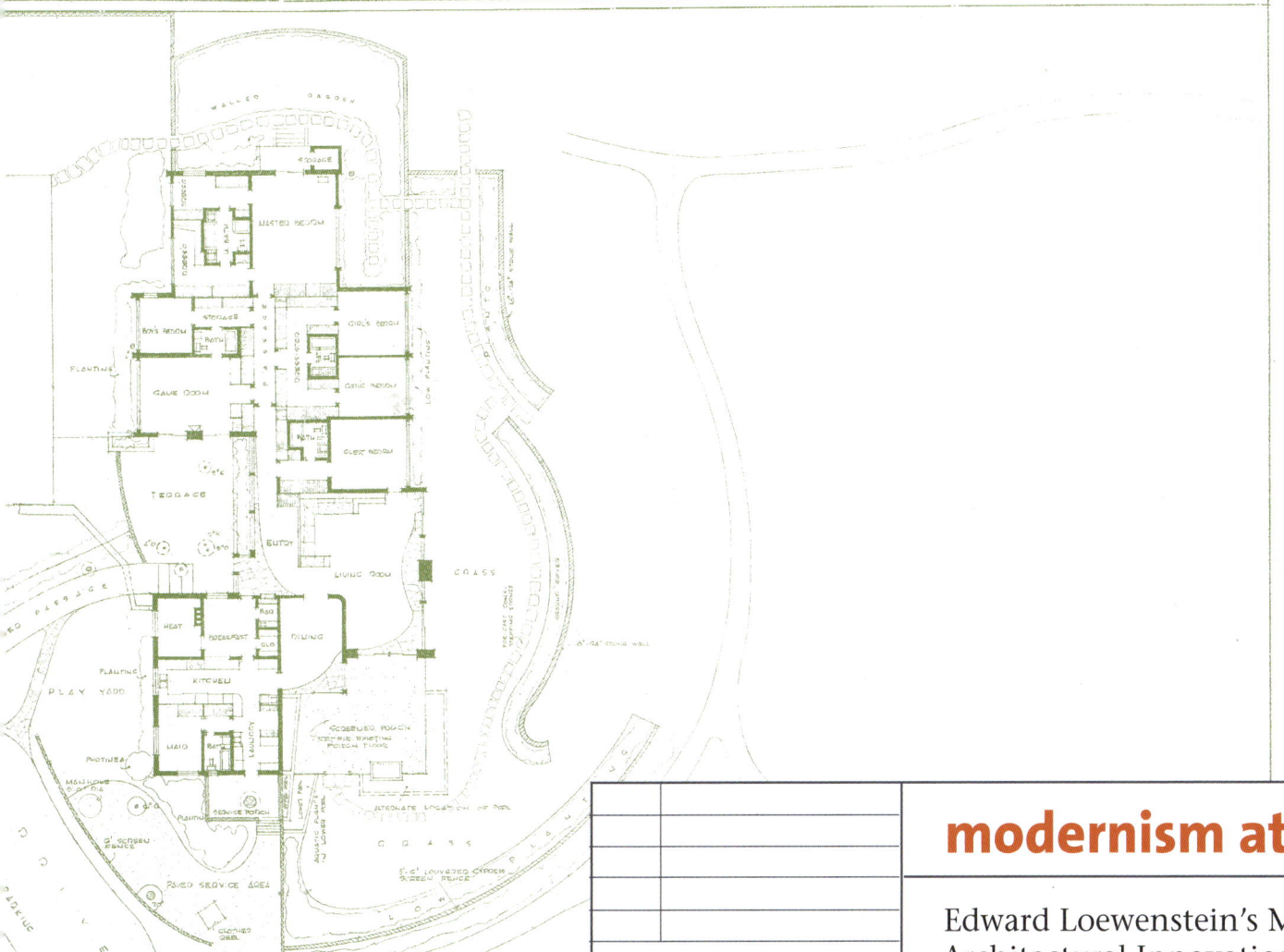

modernism at home:

Edward Loewenstein's Mid-Century Architectural Innovation in the Civil Rights Era

BY PATRICK LEE LUCAS

MODERNISM AT HOME:
Edward Loewenstein's Mid-Century Architectural Innovation in the Civil Rights Era
Published by the Weatherspoon Art Museum,
The University of North Carolina at Greensboro, 2013.

Copyright © 2013 Patrick Lee Lucas
All rights reserved.

Photos and artwork: C. Timothy Barkley Photography, *Bride's Magazine*, Danny Fafard, *Greensboro Daily News*, Jax Harmon, Loewenstein-Atkinson archive, Patrick Lee Lucas, *McCall's*, *New York Times Magazine*, *Southern Architect*, Jennifer René Tate, UNCG Special Collections and Archives, David Wilson/*UNCG Magazine*, and several private collections.
© All rights reserved.

No part of this publication may be reproduced in any form by any electronic or mechanical means (including photocopying, recording, or information storage and retrieval) without permission in writing from Patrick Lee Lucas.

ISBN: 978-0-615-86603-1
Library of Congress Control Number: 2013948566

With support from the Edward T. Cone Foundation, the Marion Steadman Covington Foundation, the Greensboro Historical Museum, Preservation Greensboro, Inc., Weatherspoon Art Museum and the University of North Carolina at Greensboro.

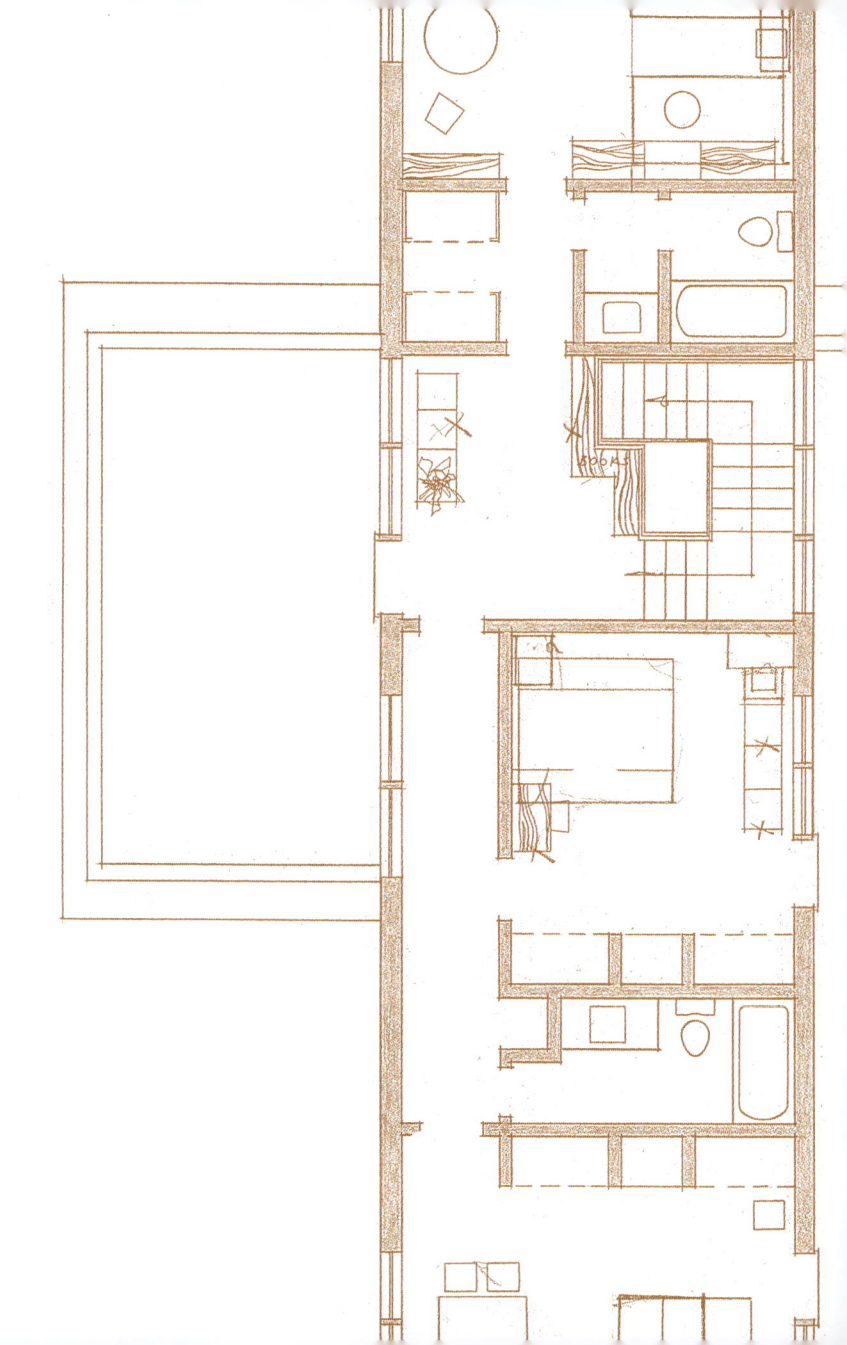

5	acknowledgements
9	foreword
10	modernism in context
24	giving form to the dream house

prototype – MARTHA + WILBUR L. CARTER, JR. RESIDENCE: Greensboro (1950–1951) | ELEANOR + MARION BERTLING RESIDENCE: Greensboro (1953)

archetype – FRANCES + EDWARD LOEWENSTEIN RESIDENCE: Greensboro (1954)

hybrid – JULIET + OSCAR BURNETT RESIDENCE: Greensboro (1954)

54	beyond plantation nostalgia

KATHERINE + SIDNEY J. STERN, JR. RESIDENCE: Greensboro (1955) | EVELYN + JOHN HYMAN RESIDENCE: Greensboro (1959) | JOANNE SPANGLER RESIDENCE: Danville (1958–1959) | JOANNE + WAYNE DAVIS RESIDENCE: Pleasant Garden (1959–1961) | BETTIE S. + ROBERT S. CHANDGIE RESIDENCE: Greensboro (1958) | BETTY + CHARLES ROTH RESIDENCE: Greensboro (1958)

82	an experiment in design education

FRANCES + IRVIN SQUIRES RESIDENCE: Greensboro (1958) | MARION + KENNETH P. HINSDALE RESIDENCE: Greensboro (1959) | NANCY + HERBERT SMITH RESIDENCE: Sedgefield (1965)

91	emerging civilities + situations

ALF HOLLAR RESIDENCE (HORIZON HOUSE): Greensboro (1962) | LEAH + A. J. TANNENBAUM RESIDENCE: Greensboro (1963) | JOAN + RICHARD STEELE RESIDENCE: Greensboro (1964) | ANNE + JAMES H. WILLIS RESIDENCE: Greensboro (1965) | JOAN + HERBERT FALK RESIDENCE: Greensboro (1966)

106	the legacy of modernism today

acknowledgements

Part of knowing any community where one resides comes in understanding its sense of place. When I moved to Greensboro in 2002, I knew precious little about this charming southern town and certainly had no knowledge of the remarkable Edward Loewenstein. In the process of undertaking the research that has yielded his design story, I have come to deeply appreciate the community where I have been privileged to live for more than a decade. As a faculty member in the Department of Interior Architecture at the University of North Carolina at Greensboro, I followed in the footsteps of Mr. Loewenstein who taught architectural history and design studios at the same institution for a decade and a half during the latter part of his life. He has provided a pathway for design excellence and served as a mentor from the past in my teaching. I can think of no better model for gentleness, innovation, and acceptance than this man who has been really more of a partner with me, rather than a subject, in telling this story about Greensboro in the decades of civil rights.

Living in Greensboro in the twenty-first century but seeing the community through Mr. Loewenstein's work in the mid-twentieth has changed the way I think about the world and what community means to people. This catalog represents the efforts of hundreds of individuals who, in one way or another, assisted with my research. I am deeply grateful for the community that has formed as a result as we all have worked together to uncover and interpret his work. That story begins with my talented colleague, Jo Ramsay Leimenstoll, who innocently asked one day in my first year at UNCG if I would like to help plan a house tour. Never before have I been so glad to say yes because, in doing so, I opened the door to learning about the career of an incredible person and the deep impact he had on anyone he encountered. Through the many people involved with the Loewenstein Legacy since its inception in 2003 to the production of this catalog, I have seen Greensboro with new eyes and have come to more deeply appreciate what one person can do to affect change. I only hope that I have helped in some small way to memorialize Mr. Loewenstein's work and to tell the story of the community where his work unfolded.

Like Edward Loewenstein, who understood the power inherent in a collective group of people working together, I have not done this alone. I am indebted to Dabney Sanders, who I learned was really the inspiration behind the first house tour as a supplementary project to the Weatherspoon Art Museum's exhibition on Gregory Ivy. Dabney, as I have come to experience, knows more than anyone how to motivate and connect community members to better the place where we live. I have truly learned much from her and express my deep thanks here for her curiosity about the Loewenstein houses which she had visited that ultimately led to the many years of happy work for me on this subject. Right at her side, Jane Loewenstein Levy helped with the Loewenstein Legacy every step of the way — from house tour and symposium to the establishment of a scholarship fund at UNCG in Edward Loewenstein's name to the development of a multi-sited exhibit and an accompanying website right through to the production of this printed work. From Jane, I have seen Greensboro through many decades in the eyes of this native daughter. Her insight and wisdom about a life lived well have benefitted me greatly as I have come to learn about her father and the opportunities in which he engaged to make Greensboro a better place. Both of these women have had a profound impact on me as a scholar and an individual and I know this project and my life have benefitted multifold from our walk on this pathway together.

This work on Loewenstein's residential architecture would not have been possible were it not for homeowners who generously opened their doors, closets, and cabinets to allow me and a host of students to better understand the physical realities of Loewenstein's designs. Though a number of the houses remain a residence for original owners, a second generation of homeowners joined in the opportunities for research and sharing many times over by enthusiastically establishing an open door policy themselves. By all of these stewards of Modernism sharing their homes so readily, I have come to enjoy their keen eyes for good design, their infectious community spirit, and their sharing of laughter and a fondness for the places they call home. My hat is off to each and every one of them: Porter Aichele and Fritz Janshcka, Liz and Bill Blackwell, Lin Bostian, W.L. Carter, Jr., Bettie and Robert Chandgie, Harvey Colchamiro, Kathy and Daniel Craft, Mrs. Burke Davis, Joanne and Wayne Davis, the Fleishman family, Danny Graves, Elaine and John Hammer, the Hinsdale family, Joan Falk Isaacson, Henry Jacobsen, Lindsey and Kody Jones, Karen and Ron Lashley, Barbara Lavietes, Jane and Richard Levy, Tammy and Slade Lewis, Fred Lopp, Betty Roth, Sara and Tom Sears, Nancy Downs Smith, Andrea and Michael Spangler, Joyce and Fred Sparling, Joan and Richard Steele, Kay Stern, Jeanne Tannenbaum, Jock Tate, Marie Tyndall, and Charles L. Weill, Jr. I recognize as well the efforts of Sue Miller and Vicky Vanstory, both realtors, who helped connect me to homeowners, and my travel partners, Richard and Jane Levy, who made innumerable field trips to see these proud stewards of mid-century design in Greensboro and beyond.

This catalog would certainly be far less interesting had I not had the opportunity, with student help, to analyze the archival records of the Loewenstein firm, a research process made possible through the generosity of Tom Wilson of Wilson & Lysiak, Inc., the firm who inherited the Loewenstein and Loewenstein-Atkinson records. Tom generously allowed open access and a remarkable dynamic duo of students and I sifted through more than fifty years of records during some hot summer months and some very cold winters in the attic of the firm's building. To April Lewis and Denise Smith I owe a tremendous debt. Their chattering teeth and spirited laughter represent some very fond memories as we re-lived the 1950s through the materials collected by the firm. I also recognize here the handiwork of Virginia Bright, Mr. Loewenstein's assistant, who grasped the importance of an organized filing system for the firm that made research on them five decades later a pleasurable task. Others who worked for the firm or enjoyed a close relationship with those who did contributed important perspectives as well: Mackie Jeffries Mcdonald Bane, Jim Brandt, Charlie Doss, Clinton Gravely, Frank Harmon, and Glenna Lewis.

I eagerly acknowledge the talent of C. Timothy Barkley, another kind man from Greensboro, whose lovely photographs of houses populate this catalog. Alongside archival photographs, drawings, and other visuals, Tim's stunning images bring the vitality of Loewenstein's designs to the viewer. Capably assisted by his wife, Miriam, he worked rapidly in two stints to achieve excellent views for the houses that you see here and I am especially thankful for his gentle manner in handling the details of photography with such ease and skill, making my life easier in the process. I acknowledge, too, the many students and other photographers who generously lent their work to make the visual part of this work so engaging. Thanks, especially, to Jax Harmon, Jennifer René Tate, and David Wilson, among others, whose work appears in these pages. Unless otherwise noted, all other images result from my limited photography skills.

Besides those already mentioned, UNCG Interior Architecture and History graduate students undertook initial investigations for the 2005 tour and symposium which form the foundation for the research in this work: Jenny Alkire, Jennifer Blakemore, Carrie Ehrfurth, Amanda Wade, and Matisha Wiggs, under the capable leadership of Ruth Little, whose survey class focused on Modernism. The undergraduates and graduates in the 2007 exhibit design studio, both from the Department of Interior Architecture and the Department of Art, and those in the 2007 material culture course, and my own history and theory class patiently and thoroughly transformed the knowledge of what we knew about Loewenstein, elevating the scholarly art of research and exhibit-making on this subject to a substantial degree. I especially recognize here my faculty colleagues in Art — Chris Cassidy, Seth Ellis, and Amy Lixl-Purcell — who took the leap of faith with me and capably guided art students through design and fabrication exercises that changed the way we all viewed the houses in the pages that follow. Of the many students involved in this phase of the Loewenstein Legacy (listed in the final chapter of this work), I single out Ashley Boycher and Gwen Mckinney, who participated in the studio project and contributed in significant ways to our information gathering and knowledge of Loewenstein far beyond that single semester.

Thanks also to Ashley Warriner Andrews, Mira Eng-Getz, Madeline Farlow, Vanessa Morehead, Leah Rowland, Maiken Schoenleber, and Denise Smith for fascinating forays as researchers (funded through the UNCG Office of Undergraduate Research) into mid-century Modernism that inform this work. I extend my heartfelt and deep appreciation to Karyn Reilly and Sally Shader Warther, who helped carry this final stage of the project to fruition in their work as leaders for the 2013 symposium and tour.

Many working in development and university relations at UNCG helped connect me with graduates from Woman's College who assisted with understanding the importance of the design and construction of the first Commencement House. Of these professionals, Jane Lawrence deserves special mention for her deep knowledge of the old home economics world and her ability to sleuth in locating alums from those important years. Thanks, too, goes to Herman Trojanowski and Betty Carter from the university's Division of Special Collections, as well as David Gwynn, Digital Projects Coordinator, all in the Walter Jackson Clinton Library, who helped uncover significant archival materials and images, some of which are used in this catalog. Finally, at UNCG, I thank Tommy Lambeth, who championed my participation in this project from conception to writing, both in his capacity at Head of the Department of Interior Architecture and as a friend and gifted colleague.

This community story increased in breadth and depth as the result of the many interviews and suggestions undertaken by students or by me, most notably those conducted with Jim Schlosser, Flo Snider, and Jim Turner, all of whom helped capture the Greensboro spirit that Edward Loewenstein himself encountered. I also acknowledge community agencies and individuals who helped along the way: Stephen Catlett, Archivist; Linda Evans, Community Historian; and Jon B. Zachman, Curator of Collections, all at the Greensboro Historical Museum; Preservation Greensboro, Inc. and its Executive Director Benjamin Briggs; the staff and leadership of the Community Foundation of Greater Greensboro; as well as Nancy Doll, Director of the Weatherspoon Art Museum and Curator Xandra Eden, all of whom contributed in important ways to this project.

Gracious colleagues, friends, and family members served as readers, editors, sounding boards, and idea people at many stages of the project and I gratefully extend my thanks to each of them who helped expand the reach of the work and the ways that we see architecture and design: Catherine Bishir, Sarah Chowning, Judith Cushman-Hammer, Ronn Daniel, Cynthia de Miranda, Travis Hicks, Sue Keith, Bettie Kerr, Jerry Leimenstoll, Jo Ramsay Leimenstoll, Jane Levy, Richard Levy, Karen Litterer, Ruth Little, Rose Moloney Lucas, Paul Manoguerra, Glenn Perkins, Mary Sertell, Stephen Swoap, and Lisa Tolbert.

Financial support to print this catalog comes from the Edward T. Cone Foundation and I value the confidence its board of trustees and officers have bestowed on the project, most notably George Pitcher and T. Randolph Harris.

A portion of the first essay appeared in an earlier form in the *Journal of Southern Jewish History* in 2013. I gratefully acknowledge the *Journal* and its generous editors for granting permission for re-use.

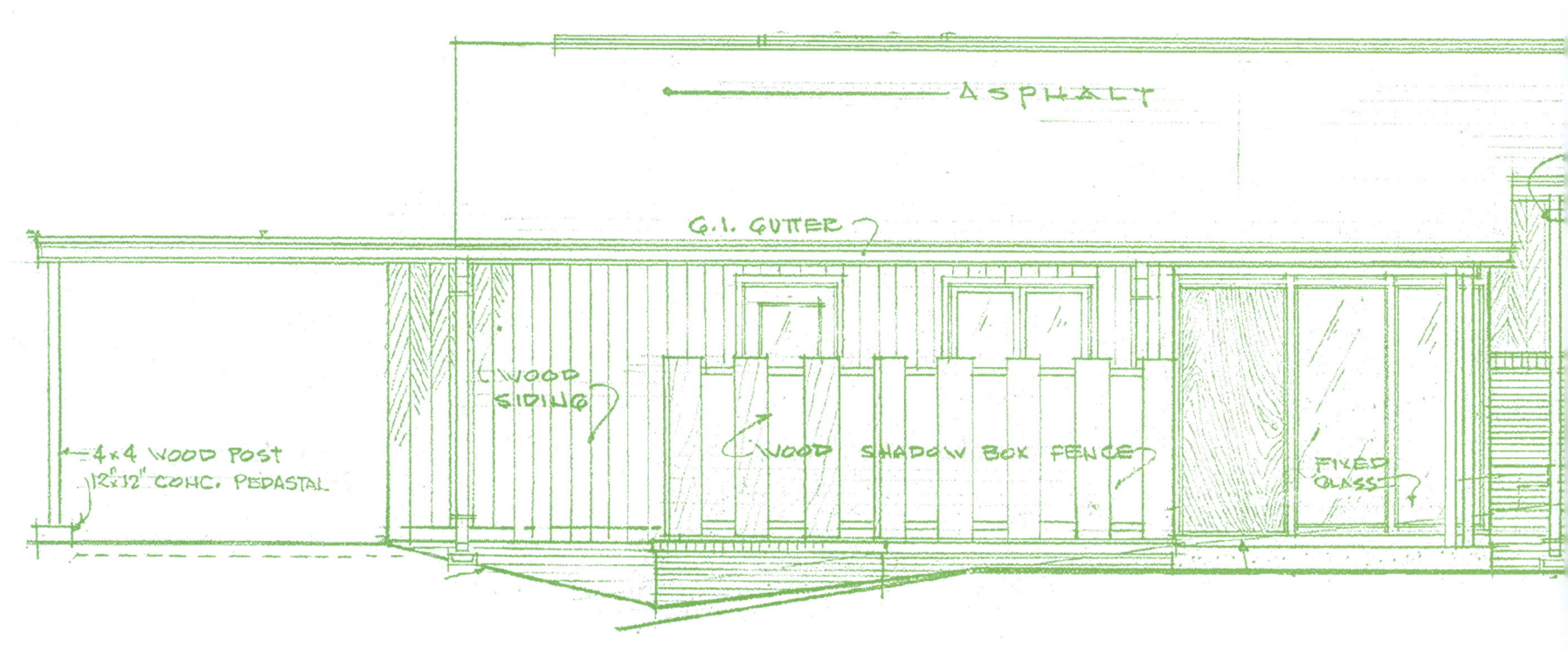

foreword

In *Modernism at Home: Edward Loewenstein's Mid-Century Architectural Innovation in the Civil Rights Era*, Patrick Lee Lucas makes an important contribution to the understanding and appreciation of mid-century modernism in North Carolina.

Mid-twentieth century North Carolina from the 1930s onward and especially during the challenging and promising years after World War II fostered a remarkable collection of this architecture, which drew upon international models together with regional themes and embodied the hopes of leaders and individuals who sought to bring new economic, educational, and social progress to the state. There were several centers of architectural progressivism. The best known is associated with the modernist School of Design at North Carolina State University in Raleigh established in 1948 — the Dorton Arena at the State Fairgrounds is the "jewel in the crown" — but there were others with other stories: California-influenced residential work in Chapel Hill; corporate and residential modernism in Charlotte; diverse expressions in western North Carolina including Black Mountain and Asheville; and as Lucas shows us, buildings in Piedmont industrial cities including Greensboro. Other individual examples appear in communities from Wilmington to Yadkinville.

In recent years, myriad North Carolinians — architects, scholars, and preservationists, homeowners and fans of the modernist esthetic — have drawn attention to the extent and value of our state's mid-century modernist heritage. At North Carolina State University Libraries, Special Collections in Architecture emphasizes architectural records associated with these buildings and their makers. Individuals and groups in Tar Heel communities, including North Carolina (formerly Triangle) Modernist Houses (NCMH) work to broaden appreciation and preservation. The North Carolina State Historic Preservation Office generates surveys and National Register of Historic Places nominations for historic modernist architecture. These efforts also raise national awareness of North Carolina's place in America's constellation of mid-century modernist architecture.

Yet at the same time, we are losing both major and modest examples of this heritage. Sometimes they fall victim to the high property values and development potential of the land on which they stand. All too often they go under the wrecking ball because private citizens and public officials have a hard time seeing the architecture of the recent past as historic, or simply do not like modernist design. The challenge is to broaden awareness and respect for this special part of the state's architectural legacy.

Patrick Lee Lucas has devoted years to researching and interpreting the career of Edward Loewenstein as Greensboro's key proponent of mid-century modernist residential architecture. The northern-born and educated Jewish architect came to the growing industrial city after marrying into its powerful Cone family of textile manufacturers, who with their relatives helped make Greensboro a center of successful Jewish life. Thus grounded, he developed a clientele among leading Jewish and gentile families alike. He modeled progressive ideals in his racially integrated architectural office, his wide range of clients, and in designs that adapted modernist concepts to the local setting. Attuned to his clients' tastes and family lives, he designed residences that ranged from pure modernism to standard "traditional" houses, with myriad "hybrids" in between. Akin to such masters as Harwell Hamilton Harris (the California regionalist who spent his later years at the School of Design in Raleigh), Loewenstein favored what Lucas terms a "gentle" and "fluid" approach to modernism, blending innovative forms and materials with familiar natural materials and a strong connection with the natural environment. As the catalog title indicates, his designs made his clients feel "at home," and in turn his houses were "at home" in their communities.

A vital step in preserving our mid-century modernist heritage for future generations to enjoy is to showcase our modernist architecture in ways that highlight its beauty and significance for a wide audience. In this volume, Lucas presents a cornucopia of photographs and drawings of these "gentle" modernist houses that fulfills this goal. May this be one of many such works that amplify appreciation for our state's special legacy from a time that reshaped our history.

Catherine W. Bishir
Curator in Special Architectural Collections
North Carolina State University Libraries
Raleigh, North Carolina

Loewenstein-Atkinson Architects, ca. 1962, Loewenstein at far left, Atkinson at far right. (Loewenstein-Atkinson archives, hereafter LAA)

modernism in context

in a community where the sit-in movement, in part, originated and where civil rights struggles marked the 1950s and 1960s, Edward Loewenstein's vernacular Modern buildings stood side by side with conventional architecture more grounded in the past. His story, which is a story of the ability of architecture and design to resonate with issues of culture, suggests that he expressed aspiration for change in the community. His work for Jewish and non-Jewish families alike helped to deliver that vision in houses that stood in contrast to those of their neighbors, houses in distinct ways that demonstrated a balanced sociological expression for their homeowners. These explorations of a localized Modern dialect stand as material evidence of a progressive designer who championed equality, mentored up-and-coming designers across race and gender lines, and actively engaged in community service to numerous civil rights and other organizations.

As an architect, Loewenstein produced buildings with social and political implication as evidence of race relations, ethnic distinction, and community values through service to others and provided service to the community through his work. As a student trained in the North, he espoused a design view quite different from the community to which he emigrated. As an employer, he hired the first African-American architects in a firm in the city. As an outsider to Greensboro who became part of a prominent Jewish family, he worked to bring a different vision of openness and acceptance of others in a community that valued the tried and true in both design and in social conventions. The language of his designs grew out of these orientations in character and geography as well as his approaches to life. Through his buildings, he quietly expressed the need for change in the face of more conservative modes and models, an expression resonating with the larger national discourse about design at mid-century.

Like other of his contemporaries, Loewenstein reinterpreted the stark Modernism of previous generations of architects, adapting a more nuanced version of the style suited to a local context, significantly a context to which he was considered an outsider. Born in Chicago in 1913, Loewenstein earned a Bachelor of Architecture degree from the Massachusetts Institute of Technology (MIT) in 1935.[1] He apprenticed in Illinois after graduation and opened a solo practice in Chicago.[2] After serving in the army during World War II, he moved to Greensboro in 1945 with his wife, Frances Stern, a Greensboro native and stepdaughter of textiles magnate, Julius Cone. Through his marriage, Loewenstein accessed a large social network of contacts within and outside of the Jewish community and secured design commissions from them and others that helped him redefine architecture in Greensboro in the post-war period.[3] He established a solo practice in 1946 that expanded in 1953 into a flourishing partnership with Robert A. Atkinson Jr., which continued until Loewenstein's untimely death in 1970.

As a Jew married into a distinguished Jewish family, Loewenstein brought a different design sensibility to Greensboro, one that borrowed from his vantage as a person growing up in the North and from his schooling in the Modernist environment at the Massachusetts Institute of Technology. In studying his first efforts in providing Modern residences, we are able to see his impact on the community. Far from making a claim here for a "Jewish architecture," his early commissions demonstrate how he helped Jewish and non-Jewish clients alike visualize alternatives and new ideas, commensurate with those written largely in the post-World War II suburbs throughout the nation. In this era, some Jews aspired to quiet dissent as they simultaneously sought a place in mainstream culture and identity.[4] Through their architecture, Jews espoused a certain cosmopolitan character rooted in the tenets of Modernism. Importantly, however, their Modern dwellings did not contain the cold and sterile interiors of the high Modernists featured in design magazines. The residences Loewenstein designed stood as softer and quieter expressions of the day, safely situating this dialect not as a distinct Southern-Jewish identity but as one of many voices in the Southern landscape whose expression helps us see and hear the social and cultural implication of Jews at home in the region.[5]

Although scholars have addressed various meanings of vernacular Modernism in mid-twentieth-century residential structures, few have investigated forward-thinking dwellings in medium-sized Southern cities, such as those designed by Loewenstein. Moreover, Loewenstein joined a community of progressively minded and socially engaged individuals who helped transform Greensboro in the 1950s and 1960s. Loewenstein's story counters the portrayal of the Gate City as a place occupied by largely ineffectual politicians and dismal social prospects for non-whites; at the very least, it complicates our notions of the community at mid-century.[6]

Far from having only a local relevance, Loewenstein's experience echoes that of other designers and architects throughout the nation, professionals who struggled to redefine suburban residential design standards in the decades after World War II with many proposing more contemporary styles. Despite these new alternatives, homeowners repeatedly selected linkages to the past, clinging to designs based largely on the Classical revivals of the nineteenth century and the Colonial buildings of the previous century. However, some forward-thinking clients hired architects and designers to bring Modernism to the suburbs. These architects visually and intellectually challenged assumptions of what a house could look like and stand for in turbulent times, beginning a design conversation of sorts in built form. If residential architecture is understood as a social act resulting in sited physical and tangible products, then mid-century Modern residences suggested a change in ideas about politics, identity, and worldview true in Greensboro and equally valid in many sections of the United States.

MENTORING BEYOND BOUNDARIES OF RACE, GENDER, AND CLASS

The firm of Loewenstein-Atkinson produced more than 1,600 commissions, one quarter of them residential. Although Loewenstein's buildings comprise a tremendous physical legacy, the architect's other great contribution to the North Carolina built environment came in the training he gave to many architects and designers who practiced throughout the state. Notably, the firm hired the first African-American architects and design professionals in Greensboro and North Carolina after World War II. The late William Street, Loewenstein's MIT classmate, who

eventually joined North Carolina A&T's faculty; the late W. Edward Jenkins, the first licensed African-American architect in Greensboro; and Clinton E. Gravely, all of whom pursued prolific architectural careers in North Carolina and beyond, counted among the first African-American professionals hired by Loewenstein's firm. In 1959, the National Conference of Christians and Jews published a booklet entitled "A Fair Chance for All Americans," in which Loewenstein wrote: "At the present time, our firm is composed of every race, breed, color, and religion with the exception of Eskimos. Our philosophy has been based on the fact that we consider everyone a member of some minority, and we have tried to treat everyone on the basis of his or her abilities and not their ancestors."[7]

Equality for Loewenstein extended beyond hiring practices. As an advocate of civil rights, the firm completed buildings for the greater good of Greensboro, including the master plan and design for twelve buildings at Bennett College, a traditionally African-American woman's campus. In addition, the firm received a 1960 Award of Excellence for Aesthetic Design by the American Institute of Steel Construction for the **Dudley High School Gymnasium** (1959), then a school for African-Americans. Loewenstein embraced underserved populations in the design for two YWCA buildings and a major addition to the YMCA, correcting the inequities in facilities and finally uniting in a single building the black and white branches that had existed separately through the 1960s.

Despite some fallout from Loewenstein's more liberal attitude toward race, the firm continued to receive admiration while striving for diversity because of the collective spirit of enterprise within its ranks and in creative association with design professionals outside the firm. Loewenstein mentored hundreds of students as interns and young hires, among them Frank Harmon of North Carolina and Anne Greene of Washington, DC, both of whom went on to design award-winning buildings and interiors throughout the United States. More than thirty

Golden Gate Shopping Center (1961). (LAA)

architects, draftsmen, and support staff worked at the firm at its peak size in the mid-1960s. As inheritors of Loewenstein's mid-century Modern aesthetic, these practitioners continued to shape architectural and design endeavors in the nation with each passing decade.

Loewenstein also taught at the Woman's College of the University of North Carolina from 1958 through the late 1960s. Loewenstein innovated an active system of learning by taking women out of the classroom and into the field of home construction. In 1957-1958, Loewenstein offered a yearlong design course, through the Department of Art and the Department of Home Economics, which attracted twenty-three students. In studio, the students designed a house, oversaw its construction, and decorated the resulting structure, dubbed the "Commencement House" by the university's public relations office. Completed in 1958, the first house was followed by two others in 1959 and 1965. The houses formed an important physical legacy that symbolized shifting gender roles in design. All three of these houses resulted from innovation espoused by Loewenstein, alongside the students, and the various partners and collaborators who made the efforts possible. The houses also represented the resiliency of Loewenstein, and the firm, to incorporate alternative approaches to the design process in a time of vast change for the community and the nation. The nonconformity of the houses, quiet in their neighborhood settings, parallels the students sit in as a form of silent protest in downtown Greensboro in 1961.

With their wide range of building types and scales, Loewenstein's commercial buildings reflected his belief in community and civic engagement. Shortly after moving to town, Loewenstein joined in temporary partnership with Greensboro architect Charles Hartmann Jr. to design the **North Carolina Convalescent Hospital** (1948) in response to a polio epidemic that swept the city and the resultant need for healthcare facilities to house those recovering from the disease. In the 1950s, Loewenstein-Atkinson designed schools, hospitals, religious buildings, and public facilities, including the award-winning Woman's College **Coleman Gymnasium** (1952) and the **David D. Jones Elementary School** (1954), the winner of a 1955 Award of Merit from the North Carolina Chapter of the American Institute of Architects.

In the more tumultuous 1960s, the firm designed the **Golden Gate Shopping Center** (1961) to provide an easily accessed store east of Elm Street for the growing populations near the Cone mill village. Through the Bessemer Land Company, Loewenstein and the firm's employees still worked in traditionally African American neighborhoods in east Greensboro. Several commissions came through Cone Mills and its related institutions, including the **Sixteenth Street Baptist Church** (ca. 1965) and school complex near the mill. The **Greensboro Public Library** (1964), perhaps Loewenstein's best-known community building stands as a symbol of progress, anchoring civic pride and the progressive spirit of the community in troubling times.[8]

Greensboro Public Library (1964). (Sketch by Patrick Lee Lucas)

JEWS AND MODERNISM IN GREENSBORO

As the only known Jewish architect practicing in North Carolina during the middle of the twentieth century, Loewenstein's work takes on great significance in understanding life as a Jew in the South, specifically one who practiced in a profession not heavily populated with Jews.[9] Outside North Carolina, Jewish architects brought to the landscape some remarkable Modern structures. Those with national or worldwide reputations, such as Gordon Bunshaft (1909–1990), Sheldon Fox (1930–2006), Bertrand Goldberg (1913–1997), Percival Goodman (1904–1989), Louis Kahn (1901–1974), and Richard J. Neutra (1892–1970), maintained prosperous careers and received significant commissions. All of these men, including Loewenstein, trained as Modernists in architecture school and embraced tenets of the design movement in their work. They all balanced views of architectural ambition

Beth Israel Synagogue, Fayetteville (1966). (LAA)

and acculturation into the mainstream.[10]

Yet few Jewish architects practiced in the South. Even in synagogue design and construction, where one might expect Jewish names to be associated, non-Jewish architects prevailed. Even fewer Jewish architects in the South espoused Modern design philosophies. Thus Loewenstein's body of work stands out distinctly from his peers in the state and region. Curiously, Loewenstein designed two synagogues, only one of which was actually built.[11] The Beth Israel Congregation in Fayetteville, North Carolina, retained Loewenstein's services, and he produced a distinctive structure with a saw-toothed roof profile. Completed in 1962, the extant building shows the masterful plays of light and shadow Loewenstein envisioned.[12] In Greensboro, although he was involved on the building committee of the Beth David Synagogue in 1966, he never received a significant commission for the edifice.[13]

Northern industrialists, among them Moses and Ceasar Cone of Baltimore, transformed Greensboro in the last part of the nineteenth century, when they began to build textile plants.[14] By 1900, many considered Greensboro the center of the Southern textile industry, with its large-scale factories producing denim, flannel, and overalls.[15] By the mid-twentieth century, the Cone Corporation's five plants in Greensboro produced many types of cloth, and the firm was attributed the title of the world's largest manufacturer of denim, supplying denim for Levi's jeans both before and after World War II. In Greensboro, the Cones encountered a progressive community accepting of their religious views. Family and city "grew up together," with the Cones helping the community and the community helping the Cones.[16] Eli Evans posited, "Greensboro is unique for the contribution of the Cone family. That sets it apart from other cities in the South."[17] Zeigenhaft and Comhoff concur, writing, "for the past 75 years, the Jews of Greensboro have lived in a town where among the most prominent, wealthy, and visible people has been a Jewish family named Cone."[18]

As leaders, the Cones made significant philanthropic efforts and encouraged other Jewish families to similarly dedicate themselves to the well-being of the community. In the administration of the cultural and social life of Cone plant workers in the mill villages, and through significant donations to particular education and recreational pursuits, politics, and the arts, the Jews in Greensboro formed a part of the community but did not stand apart from it.[19] Although Jews helped shape communities throughout the South from the last decades of the nineteenth century (and in many cases, much earlier), in Greensboro the breadth of the Cone holdings and their ability to shape the municipality bore out over time architecturally in the construction of buildings that carry their name, notably the Cone Building on the campus of the University of North Carolina at Greensboro, Moses Cone Hospital, Cone Elementary School, and the Cone Building owned by the City of Greensboro, as well as the award-winning **Cone Textiles Laboratory Building** (1952), designed by Loewenstein. That Loewenstein married into this powerful family suggests he certainly had an insider's view of the order of the community. Although he did little residential work directly for the Cones, Loewenstein's relationship with the family mattered in the mid-century socio-cultural politics of Greensboro.[20]

Jews in Greensboro, as elsewhere in the South, represented a liberal faction within mainstream groups of the town. Horowtiz characterizes Greensboro Jews as sympathetic to but not overly active in civil rights for "fear that their contract with the white Gentiles might be broken" and for "fear of retribution."[21] Despite this fear, many Jews found Greensboro a hospitable community, although it was the Jews who had to be able to integrate and interweave their lives with non-Jews. Horowitz indicates that "Jews of Greensboro knew that social acceptance rested on diminishing differences rather than highlighting them," including marriage to non-Jews.[22] Loewenstein went beyond most others in his social and ethnic group by hiring young black architects and treating them equally. With the connections between him and civil rights, one may assume that Bennett College leaders commissioned Loewenstein to undertake fifteen separate jobs at the institution as a kind of testimony to his clear stand on race, and not because of his Cone relations.[23]

Because of his contacts in the business and social spheres of the town, made possible in part through the Cone network, Loewenstein attracted clients across ethnic and racial groups. Thus his design work operated both within and outside the Jewish community, much like the range of design solutions he offered to homeowners from traditional to Modern. Of his two-dozen Modern residences, Loewenstein planned roughly half for Jews and half for non-Jews.[24] In the total number of commissions for his firm, however, Jews built more Modern structures compared to non-Jews, with nearly 40% preferring something other than traditional structures as compared to 25% of the non-Jewish clientele. These numbers reveal a predilection among Loewenstein's Jewish clients for a building that stands out more than one that fits in with neighbors. With his low-key (or soft) approach to Modernism, Loewenstein offered functional and practical homes that sat quietly on their lots and did not intrude in their neighborhoods. Rather than overtly demonstrate tenets of high Modernism (or a more academic version of Modernism), he helped homeowners to fit in with their neighbors in a nontraditional manner. Perhaps Jews modulating between acculturation and distinctiveness opted to gently state difference through the architecture of their homes, as a gesture toward cosmopolitan ways.

Loewenstein's practice reflected the broader customs in architecture across the United States at the time by working to negotiate the needs of clients who desired both Modern and traditional structures.[25] The houses he designed might be thought of as a kind of conversation, with certain questions embedded within them about what to say and to whom. Imagine a mid-century conservative Southern town that, like many, grappled

Cone Textiles Laboratory (1952). (LAA)

Coleman Gymnasium, Woman's College of the University of North Carolina (1954). (UNCG Special Collections and Archives, hereafter UNCG-SCA)

with race and difference. Loewenstein's architectural lexicon of a humanist Modernism spoke a language of acceptance to new things (materials, compositions, features, furnishings) and new ideas (open planning, connecting landscape and interior). The architecture of most houses in the community, with their white columns and traditional fronts, spoke to conformity with tradition and a certain obscurity of questions about race and class behind well-ordered, balanced, and symmetrical façades. Loewenstein's Modern structures represented progressive ideas considering the choices of the day and challenged conventions in house building as well as in human identity. In the same manner that he devised more equal hiring practices for his firm, he actively worked out how to reconcile the traditions of his profession with the innovations possible in the post-war era. He developed his design language by literally living with and within the buildings he created and by engaging in his community through both his ideas and his practice. Imperfect as it was, that discourse equated with the real questions confronting the community about how people encounter one another and the distinctions they draw out of their commonality.

The range of styles of Loewenstein's buildings reflects a spectrum of viewpoints in the community about unity and diversity. These structures suggest that the families who lived in them had the same needs as their neighbors (living spaces, sleeping spaces, food preparation spaces, utility spaces), but Loewenstein organized those spaces in different ways depending on the orientation of the family and their ability to absorb an architectural design that did not conform with the majority. Similarly, people in the community (and Loewenstein among them) spoke about organizing the community and the people within it in a different way. Much like the buildings Loewenstein placed on the land, he quietly drew together whites and blacks within his drafting room and continued to challenge racial mores in the community through his civic service.[26] He did not have a perfect language or solution to the challenges either of architecture or of segregated culture. His buildings and his leadership characterized an individual who was working out what it meant to be an outsider in a southern community, a Jew accepting and promoting changes that came through civil rights.

Loewenstein's architectural story and the story of his liberal politics and identity represent one way that Jews in the South acculturated in the mid-twentieth century. As the nation reorganized after World War II, with the suburbs providing the place for the lion's share of this expansion, this Jew encountered a community and a state filled with tradition that espoused different views about ways to see the world. As indicated above, his work represents an incomplete story in the sense that the buildings stand in as the material record of Loewenstein working things out. Most homeowners did not record their thinking in writing. Thus we have to rely instead on the architecture to show us the differences suggested by Loewenstein and others like him from around the nation. That Loewenstein was a Jewish architect practicing in the south, active in the community, and championing civil rights makes this a story well worth telling.

COSMOPOLITAN RESIDENTIAL ARCHITECTURE

Although commercial commissions dominated the firm's job lists, residential commissions represent Loewenstein's greatest contribution to the emerging contemporary architectural lexicon of the Piedmont, where he created more than 400 livable houses on the local landscape. He also supervised a team of designers who adopted a wide range of design approaches. Reflective of his decades in practice, Loewenstein maneuvered through the polarized squabbles captured within the pages of architectural journals and design magazines over traditional and Modern structures. He designed both, rather than exclusively one or the other, working with ease across stylistic genres.

Designing with a diverse clientele including key leaders of the Jewish community, Loewenstein communicated difference in this combination of innovative and traditional buildings.[27] One approach spoke of an alternative vision for living, embracing the openness and promise of the future through Modern expression, a certain cosmopolitan character standing in bold relief to the columned mansions of the past. The other, larger, voice spoke to tradition: residential houses with Classical and Colonial Revival details and features melded with the emerging Ranch form. A third architectural voice, one of hybridization, blended traditional and Modern approaches in the same building, what Robert Maxwell terms as a "hybrid" structure in this fluid time for residential design.[28] In other words, an hybrid building might initially look as though it conformed to the tradition but, in fact, hid Modernist wings, rooms, and details from the street.

In this catalog, the reader experiences houses primarily of the first voice: Loewenstein's Modernist dwellings. These commissions reveal Loewenstein's fluid understanding among styles rather than the series of single-minded approaches often equated with Modernism. Also apparent are the voices of Loewenstein's clients as they worked with the architect to determine the best ways for themselves and their families to make their homes at mid-century. Sometimes these practices of making home indicated quiet dissent, as clients and design professionals together shaped a different way of thinking that symbolized cultural shifts of the 1950s and 1960s, the same shifts that ultimately brought four men to the Woolworth's counter in downtown Greensboro.

Loewenstein's career shows his difficult position as a progressive architect in a city with profoundly traditional stylistic and social views. Far more than a tactic for survival, his gentle approach to design and fluid boundaries among stylistic choices made him a popular and, for a time, the only architect in Greensboro to whom clients could turn without fear of being shunned in desiring one kind of house over another. Time and again, original owners, clients, and collaborators spoke of Loewenstein's gentle manner and design approaches, in great contrast to his his imposing physical stature at a height of 6'5". His effective work, reflecting a conflicted era in design and turbulent time in society, nevertheless demonstrates a keen understanding of the human condition and the ability of one architect to gently, but firmly, weave himself into the fabric of a community.[29]

GREENSBORO, THE MID-CENTURY CITY

The Greensboro that Loewenstein encountered in the late 1940s experienced similar incredible growth of other mid-sized cities of the post-war era, including a tremendous housing boom that wrought significant changes in cities and family life. The community also hosted the Overseas Replacement Depot, where the United States Army developed 650 acres of land in east Greensboro from 1943 to 1946. When the Depot closed, the government sold the land back to Cone Mills, resulting in the development of neighborhoods and shopping areas for that side of the city. To the west and the north, similar neighborhoods and shopping areas developed along West Friendly Avenue and Battleground Avenue, reflecting the impact of government programs like the GI Bill and FHA loans, and the corresponding consumer culture that grew out of these programs.

An axonometric drawing from the Loewenstein-Atkinson archives of the O.F. Stafford Residence: Sedgefield (1958), an example of the firm's traditional residential work. (LAA)

17

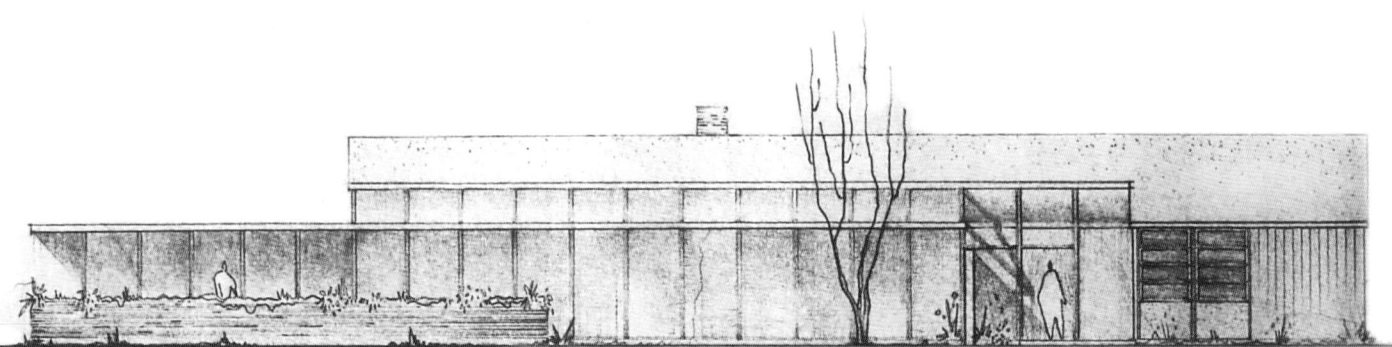

Ostensibly Loewenstein's prototype Modern dwelling — and his first in Greensboro — the Martha and Wilbur L. Carter, Jr. Residence (1950-51), took shape as a series of low lying vertical windows under a sweeping horizontal roof form, working around existing trees on its Irving Park neighborhood site. Loewenstein prepared both a traditional and modern scheme for the couple who ultimately elected the more contemporary treatment. (LAA)

Throughout the country, veterans returning from war and countless others turned outward from the urban core to land at the edges of urban settlements, fashioning new social hierarchies by occupying the landscape in predominately horizontal houses on sprawling lots. The resultant neighborhoods and their attendant commercial areas provided new structure for American communities and families largely based on gender roles, mobility, and compartmentalization in both class and race. The changes intertwined with aspects of the race struggles of the 1960s. In a period of roughly twenty years, what people wanted in their new "dream" houses, how architects and others designed them, how designers furnished and modified them, how residents lived in them, and how homeowners paid for them dramatically shifted in this suburban milieu. As Loewenstein's work unfolded, he responded to client needs across a wide range of budgets, site conditions, and emerging architectural opportunities in shaping a variety of houses.

Although population growth and the corresponding need for city services faced Greensboro, race relations represented the main issue of the 1950s and 1960s, as was certainly true of many cities throughout the south. The tensions sewn in the community, reaching far back to the nineteenth century and before, manifested in myriad ways, including the struggle for black representation on the Greensboro City Council (achieved in 1951) and the Guilford County School Board (achieved in 1954); the integration of schools (beginning at Gillespie Park Elementary School in 1957 and continuing for the next several decades); and the sit-in demonstrations at the Elm Street Woolworth's and throughout the downtown (in February 1961) and in subsequent years throughout the community. In this rocky political time, Edward Loewenstein advocated for social change by serving within civic organizations and by hiring the first African-American design professionals in a Greensboro architecture firm.

The residences Loewenstein designed, like those in other communities across the nation, stood as symbols of shifting family and community values and, particularly because of their location on the edges of cities, as places of separation from the dirty and competitive business world and from others who were different in socio-economic class and race.[31] Increasingly freed from the strictures of the Victorian world of their parents and grandparents, families refashioned their houses as places of retreat to "protect and strengthen the family, shoring up the foundations of society and instilling the proper virtues needed to preserve the republic."[32] For some, suburban residences and the suburbs would form the new moral center of the nation, enabling Americans to secure a bit of economic prosperity and an investment in the future, thus partly counteracting the Communist threat of the Cold War.[33] For others, the powerful transformation of domestic space and place related to the quest for single-family homeownership, where would-be homeowners applied for assistance from the federal government regulation and loan subsidies and where the G.I. Bill and Levittown-type developments facilitated the process of constructing the suburbs. Of course, many Americans at the time could not afford a freestanding single-family home. Under the aegis of federal government regulation of loans, homeowners (many of them veterans) applied for assistance, shifting the climate of the suburbs to one of investment with the single-family house at the center of the equation. In contrast to the reality of the ever-moving American, the suburban residence symbolized financial and political stability and permanence.[34]

Edward Loewenstein's clients espoused and encapsulated many of these views concerning race, class, gender, mobility, morality, and democracy. Shortly after she retained his design services, Joanne Spangler wrote to Loewenstein, "We must not get forced into conventionality by the builders here. We'll just have to talk them into doing it the way we want — and reasonably. After all, they've got to learn how to build by the new and better ways."[35] In Starmount Forest, a 1950s neighborhood in Greensboro with largely traditional houses, one owner submitted plans for review in 1963 and, hearing from the development leadership that they were to be "rejected for being too Modern," successfully leveraged political clout through her family to force through the contemporary design.[36] As the United States poised for political, cultural, and social leadership on the world stage, these Greensboro residents, like their counterparts throughout the nation, became arbiters of shifting tastes and sensibilities regarding the American home, though they did so along different stylistic paths. Loewenstein, like other architects, helped to define the taste of his clients situated in the particular circumstances of a Piedmont textiles town, bringing change to that community incrementally through both his traditional and Modern design work.

A QUIET VOICE OF CHANGE

Edward Loewenstein designed his earliest Greensboro houses in private practice on his own. But as demand for his work increased and as the firm evolved, Loewenstein and his partner, Atkinson, took on junior designers and draftsmen. He also worked with a varied network of interior designers, lighting designers, and contractors willing to carry forward the vision of Modern architecture, traditional dwelling, and houses in between. Loewenstein's ideas that matured in his residential Modern work over two decades distinguish his work in the more humanist or warm strain of Modernism, echoing and reinterpreting the work of their European and American Modernist mentors. Thus these houses stood like others of their ilk across the United States as an expression of cultural values. In each house, the family espoused a new design vision for home life that spoke of new relationships among family members, servants, and visitors to the American home. They traded the formal, hierarchical relationships of more traditional styles and forms for more fluid interrelationships among the people and the various spaces within

The Bessemer Land Company Office Building (1953–54), designed by Loewenstein-Atkinson, stood on ORD property as it was returned to private hands. The building won a 1955 Award of Merit from the North Carolina Chapter of the American Institute of Architects and was published in *Architectural Record* on commercial buildings in May 1953. Loewenstein wrote to the editor: "The new building is located on East Bessemer Avenue in a rapidly growing industrial and commercial area which was at one time an Army ORD base, but has been returned to private ownerships. The office building itself is completely air conditioned for year round comfort, and as the building faces southwest, the sun shade at the office windows has proven very effective."[30] (LAA)

Edward Loewenstein, ca. 1955, Martin Studios portrait. (Private collection)

the building, and they did so in a manner that, at least according to one source, remained true to a sense of Southern graciousness. With these houses, Loewenstein, along with firm employees, interior designers, consultants, and contractors spoke in a dialect that diverged from but also built on notions of Southern regionalism.

In planning traditional structures, Loewenstein and his firm demonstrated agility in copying the past as an easy link for clients to fit in with their neighbors — and the traditions of Greensboro. His Modern dwellings, alternatively, relied on a different design voice with another vocabulary: large glass windows, window walls, and sliding doors to connect inside and outside as well as the introduction of color, texture, and visual interest in rooms largely stripped of traditional décor and finishes. Working with designers who generally mixed furniture styles rather than specifying the purity of a single style, Loewenstein's architecture provided room for inherited antiques alongside mid-century Modern furnishings. Such eclecticism allowed dwellers to embrace both past and present within their environment and to both stand out and fit in with their neighbors — a quiet form of non-conformism adopted by some house owners of the mid-century.

Through his more Modern designs, Loewenstein represented both a dissenting voice in the design community and made manifest the nonconformist spirit of clients who elected to differ in their ways of life from the largely traditional neighborhoods in which they resided. Somewhere in between, Loewenstein introduced Modernism to a tradition-loving community by designing hybrid houses that lived comfortably between two worlds. These hybrid houses help others to understand multiple Modernisms, regional and local variations on international themes, rather than a single Modernism without context, site condition, or client.

Although the community of Greensboro and the greater Piedmont region provide the site for many of Loewenstein's commissions, his local story links to the national scene of mid-century suburbanization in the United States where many communities dealt with the housing boom in the decades after World War II. Everywhere, architects and designers struggled with a variety of options for appropriate design philosophy and practice. Loewenstein, like others, translated and reinterpreted the stark Modernism of the previous generations of architects and brought to the American landscape a more nuanced version of the style situated intimately in the local context of a community struggling for its identity in a post-war world. Just as others found themselves embroiled in political and social issues, Loewenstein's support for civil rights and community engagement placed him squarely within the framework of the community's debate about race relations, again linked to a national discourse.

In his Modern residences particularly, but in houses of all three genres — Modern, traditional, and hybrid — Loewenstein brought a well-grounded regional touch through the use of warm and animated materials, utilizing local brick, slate, and Carolina fieldstone to soften the Modern structures in their immediate context. He successfully paired these materials with more progressive ones — steel, glass, and plastic — and, with his designer-collaborators, specified finishing touches with decorative and textured wallpapers, textile-clad windows, and furniture that crossed stylistic genres. He embraced sophisticated, multivalent strategies for natural and electric lighting to bring architectural interest and support human life within his dwellings. Following his convention to separate public and private areas in the overall organizational scheme, an often L-shaped plan included spacious living rooms and dining rooms, along with kitchen and servant spaces in flowing and interlocking rooms that blurred boundaries between interior and exterior. In contrast, built-in storage units closed vistas to bedrooms, dividing space and reducing the amount of required freestanding furniture, all the while linking each private space to a linear, connecting hallway. Loewenstein situated his Modern houses on wooded lots, with the house entrance hidden from the road, and with outdoor rooms of landscaping materials to further underscore fluid boundaries across the building envelope from interior to exterior. Through the incorporation of these features, sometimes in contrast with traditional modes and styles and sometimes melded directly to these more conservative forms, Loewenstein and his clients brought an avant-garde cultural and social agenda to the Piedmont. He created a design aesthetic that linked aspiring ideas about Modernism both to the local circumstances of his buildings and to the universal struggles with Modern buildings in the world beyond.

In a lecture he delivered at the Woman's College, Loewenstein offered his perspective on Modern architecture: "the reasoning and thinking behind contemporary architecture as compared to traditional [is that] we are in a transition, a confused state and much is not good." He listed freedom of design, materials, and masses, and flexibility as advantages of Modern work while acknowledging the strangeness of Modern work and the likelihood that issues "crop up more in new and untried" in such forward-thinking dwellings. What followed in the speech was Loewenstein's own ideas about house design, a manifesto of sorts, that provides an excellent outline to understanding his residential work (see sidebar). Notably, Loewenstein closes the list in espousing his human-centered practice of design by linking the design process to the ultimate users for best effect.

Edward Loewenstein's second-generation Modernist work echoes similar philosophies and outputs of a wide number of designers in other communities across the South and throughout the United States. His buildings thus provide a sound source upon which to elaborate a story of consequence that links to other work. Importantly, he is the only architect working in the community in the 1950s and 1960s whose individual and firm approach embraced Modernism in the residential design sphere. Because nearly all his residential commissions of significance stood within Guilford County and the surrounding Piedmont, and given the well-documented history of Greensboro in civil rights literature, examining his buildings as particular cultural products provides additional layers to understanding the community's character. Loewenstein's story enriches our knowledge of a local community dealing with real issues and concerns in a time of great change — and gives us a more complete reading of civil rights as understood away from the Woolworth's lunch counter.

tomorrow's house...

...will be bigger
...can follow any style
...easier to run and cost less to maintain
...will reflect better architect and builder teamwork
...will make smarter use of color, both inside and out
...will be cooler in summer and warmer in winter
...will have wider overhangs
...will be better integrated with the land
...will include far more built ins such as beds, bureaus, dressing tables, bookcases, dining tables and benches...
...will provide more sheltered space for outdoor living
...will make far better use of fences or planting screens
...will be basementless (but must have a basement equivalent all purpose space above ground)
...will include more split levels
...will have a garage and carport that do double duty, be for people as well as cars
...is much more likely to have an open kitchen
...should include as many labor-saving appliances as possible
...will need more adequate wiring
...will give more thought to noise control
...must provide better planned storage...and much more of it
...will take advantage of all the new construction economies
...must be designed with more thought to how people will want to live in it[37]

notes

1. At MIT, Loewenstein encountered a program in flux. In 1931, MIT introduced a studio in gestalt principles as the foundation for "a five-year course designed to educate artists and engineers for greater public service," according to architect William Emerson, head of the program. "Massachusetts Institute of Technology President's Report" (1931), p. 17. The change in the structure of the program required that Loewenstein complete a senior thesis project and he undertook the design for a new boathouse for MIT along the Charles River. The thesis he delivered included one large 30" x 60" cover sheet in ink on linen, along with eight supplementary sheets at 24" x 36", delineating a modern two-story structure. Reflecting Loewenstein's personal interest in boating, the functional design demonstrated an acceptance of modernism by the student. *MIT Museum Archives*.

2. After completing his studies, Loewenstein first apprenticed in Illinois for Ralph E. Stoezel, Architect in 1935 and Newhouse and Bernham Architects in 1936-1937. He established his own practice in Illinois as Edward Loewenstein Architect, 1937-1941, with mainly residential commissions in Chicago and Highland Park. *American Institute of Architects Directory* (1956) p. 339. The three extant Highland Park houses all followed design tenets grounded in traditional vocabulary, suggesting the young architect's ability to work across stylistic genres, a practice he continued in Greensboro.

3. Like Jews in several North Carolina towns and cities throughout the South, Jews in Greensboro figured prominently in the early history of the community. Their legacy as merchants, community organizers, textiles factory owners, and philanthropists through community foundations cannot be underestimated. According to Leonard Rogoff, Jews in North Carolina experienced an intertwined relationship with African-Americans in the state as blacks supported Jewish business as outsiders. Driving the economy of many towns, Jews who settled in Greensboro, including Moses Cone, involved themselves in the tobacco and cotton mill industries. Rogoff, *Down Home: Jewish Life in North Carolina* (Chapel Hill, NC, 2010).

4. Eli Evans posits the idea of a unique "Southern Jewish consciousness" in his overview history of Jews in the South. First published in 1973, the author weaves together story telling, autobiography, and interpretive history to recount Jewish histories from the earliest immigrants to the present day. Evans, *The Provincials: A Personal History of Jews in the South* (Chapel Hill, NC, 1997).

5. Lee Shai Weissbach's analysis of Kentucky synagogues represents the lone volume of study connecting cultural values and Jews in the South. Centered largely on the nineteenth- and twentieth-century synagogue structures in small towns, this pictorial record documents variety and significance in these structures and the architectural and cultural stories they tell. Weissbach, *The Synagogues of Kentucky: Architecture and History* (Lexington, KY, 2011).

6. William H. Chafe, *Civilities and Civil Rights: Greensboro, North Carolina, and the Black Struggle for Freedom* (New York, 1980).

7. National Conference for Christians and Jews, "A Fair Chance for All Americans" (1959).

8. A more abbreviated version of Loewenstein's biography can be found on *North Carolina Builders and Architects: A Biographical Dictionary*, a website maintained by the North Carolina State University Libraries, http://ncarchitects.lib.ncsu.edu.

9. Only two other known Jewish architects practiced in North Carolina, but both did so before the middle of the twentieth century. Alfred S. Eichberg (1859–1921) in Wilmington was "regarded as one of the first, if not the first, Jewish architects practicing in the Deep South." Eugene John Stern (dates unknown) practiced only a handful of years from 1908 to 1915 in Charlotte, having formed with Oliver Duke Wheeler (1864–1952) and C. F. Galliher (dates unknown) the firm Wheeler, Galliher, and Stern, succeeded by the firm, Wheeler and Stern, before emigrating to Arkansas, where he formed a firm with George R. Mann (1856–1939). *NC Architects and Builders*, http://ncarchitects.lib.ncsu.edu (accessed 18 February 2013).

10. Stanley Tigerman positions these Jews, among others, as outsiders who had both the liberty and the business acumen to challenge conventional notions about architecture and design, drawing parallels between Jewish history and architectural ambition. By contrast, Gavriel Rozenfeld indicates that Modern buildings of the mid-century did not contain Jewish traits or features, rather markedly staying with the confines of Modernism as understood throughout the nation. This challenging view suggests that acculturation more readily explains the behaviors of Jewish architects. Tigerman, *The Architecture of Exile* (New York, 1988); Rosenfeld, *Building after Auschwitz: Jewish Architecture and the Memory of the Holocaust* (New Haven, CT, 2011).

11. Loewenstein served on the building committee of Temple Emmanuel and performed design services for a number of changes to the structure, including the development for an educational wing. He drew plans for a new temple in Greensboro that never materialized.

12. Note and description from Gregory Ivy to Loewenstein, 1962. Loewenstein-Atkinson Architects archives, private collection, Greensboro NC (hereafter LAA).

13. Loewenstein-Atkinson Job List, compiled 2007 from LAA. Oral tradition indicates that Loewenstein may have designed an addition to the Beth-David Synagogue in Greensboro, but no conclusive evidence has materialized to confirm this assertion.

14. Arnett, *Greensboro, North Carolina: The County Seat of Guilford* (Chapel Hill, NC, 1955), 171–174.

15. Gayle Hicks Fripp, *Greensboro, a Chosen Center* (Woodland Hills, CA, 1982) 59.

16. Marcia R. Horowitz, "The Jewish Community of Greensboro: Its Experience in a Progressive Southern City" (Master's Thesis, University of North Carolina at Greensboro, 1993), 61.

17. *Greensboro News and Record*, 27 September 1981

18. Richard L. Zweigenhaft and G. William Domhoff, *Jews in the Protestant Establishment* (New York, 1982), 77.

19. The Cone family joined the Sternbergers, Sterns, Schiffmans, and others as charter members of the Greensboro Hebrew Congregation, uniting Orthodox and Reformed assemblies in one facility. Arnett, *Greensboro*, 139. Jews also donated money for school buildings, the major hospital in town, and civic structures, besides establishing both the Weatherspoon Art Museum and the Eastern Music Festival.

20 Loewenstein designed a house each for Sydney Cone, Jr., Ceasar Cone II, and Clarence Cone, as well as numerous minor projects to several additional Cone family houses. In terms of the Cone businesses, Loewenstein only received one commission, a research building on the White Oak plant property. During construction of the Ceasar Cone house, Cone fell out with Loewenstein over whether the house should be air-conditioned. Loewenstein advocated the more forward-thinking approach: installing the system. This level of disagreement represented a rarity in client relations for Loewenstein, in that everyone else regarded Loewenstein a soft-spoken gentleman who always gave the client what he wanted (Richard and Joan Steele interview, September 2007).

21 Horowitz, "Jewish Community of Greensboro," 36, 56.

22 Ibid., 107.

23 Loewenstein's mother-in-law, Laura Weill Stern Cone, descendant of a distinguished Wilmington family, provided leadership and financial support to a number of progressive organizations and cases in civil rights and women's rights, including service as a trustee to Bennett College, an African-American woman's school. No direct evidence in the firm's or the college's archives indicates that Mrs. Cone influenced the selection of Loewenstein as architect of record for the commissions at Bennett. "Mrs. Laura Weill Cone, 81, Dies After 2-Week Illness," *Greensboro Daily News*, 5 February 1970.

24 Jewish families in Greensboro numbered 300 in 1948. Horowitz, "Jewish Community of Greensboro." Loewenstein designed houses for 11% of the Jewish population (34 commissions) in contrast to less than 1% of the non-Jewish population at mid-century.

25 Edward Paxton prepared a pamphlet for the Housing and Home Finance Agency in which he summarized 41 surveys about home ownership and design in the postwar era. Published by the U.S. Department of Commerce in 1955, the pamphlet offers brilliant insight to the mindset of the homeowner at mid-century. In an overview to the surveys, Paxton reported that 42% preferred to build a new house, rather than occupy an old one, with three-quarters of the population preferring a single-story rather than multiple-story dwelling. The owners of these new houses, according to a number of the surveys, divided in opinion about the appearance of their homes. A University of Illinois Small Homes Council Survey documented that one-third of respondents favored Modern dwellings in 1945, with a slight increase to 42% by 1946. The 1944 *McCall*'s survey, "Architectural Home of Tomorrow," indicated a slightly higher preference of 44% who wanted a Modern-style home, leaving 56% to claim more traditional houses. A 1948–1949 *Better Homes & Garden* survey demonstrated the popularity of Modern buildings west of the Mississippi River as 59% of the readers in the West Central region and 65% in the Pacific region indicated a preference for non-traditional dwellings. By contrast in New England, 64% of homeowners preferred traditional styles (including Cape Cod and Colonial). Notably, the South as a region remained unreported.

26 William J. Gupple, Jr. told Jane Loewenstein Levy the story about her father admonishing white employees who complained about the integrated drafting room. He recounted that when an unnamed employee griped, Loewenstein retorted, "if you don't like it, get the hell out," a contrast to his otherwise gentle ways. Gupple interview with Jane Levy, Greensboro, NC, March 2005.

27 Harry Golden suggests that a Jewish subculture flourished in the Carolinas at mid-century, with a tendency toward a slow acculturation and delicate balance in the context of communities. Edward S. Shapiro indicates the same sort of balance on the national scene, connecting Jews with the calamitous events of World War II and its aftermath as well as the civil rights movement. Arthur A. Goren reminds us that the Jews' exodus from the urban to suburban landscape in the late 1940s and early 1950s expressed a new influence as a rising Jewish middle class. Golden, *Jewish Roots in the Carolinas: A Pattern of American Philo-Semitism* (Greensboro, NC, 1955), 55-56; Shapiro, *We Are Many: Reflections on American Jewish History and Identity* (Syracuse, NY, 2005); Goren, *The Politics and Public Culture of American Jews* (Bloomington, IN, 1999).

28 Under a design lineage, Maxwell indicates that architects and designers work with prototypes, yielding a series of hybrids, experimenting in form and detail until the design professional arrives at an achetype. At this time, the archetype becomes the new protoype for the next phase of design in an overlapping, ever-contested cycle. Robert A. Maxwell, *Polemics: The Two-way Stretch: Modernism, Tradition, and Innovation* (London, 1996).

29 Active in the community, Loewenstein served the Cerebral Palsy Association, the Evergreens Retirement Home, the Greensboro Chamber of Commerce, the YMCA, the Greensboro Preservation Society, the Weatherspoon Association, and the local modern art museum. He was also president of the North Carolina Architectural Foundation from 1953 to 1958, the editor of *Southern Architect*, a statewide publication geared to practicing architects, and president of the Greensboro Registered Architects. The latter linked him to the North Carolina American Institute of Architects and to colleagues around the state.

30 Loewenstein to James S. Hornbeck, 2 March 1953, LAA.

31 John Archer, *Architecture and Suburbia: From English Villa to American Dream House*, 1690–2000 (Minneapolis, MN, 2005).

32 Clifford E. Clark, *The American Family Home, 1800–1960* (Chapel Hill, NC, 1986), 238.

33 Rosalyn Baxandall and Elizabeth Ewen address this theme in *Picture Windows: How the Suburbs Happened* (New York, 2000). For a more extended discussion of suburban development, see Dolores Hayden, *Redesigning the American Dream: Gender Housing, and Family Life*, 2nd ed. (New York, 2002), and Gwendolyn Wright, *Building the Dream: A Social History of Housing in America* (New York, 1981).

34 Andrew M. Shanken, *194X: Architecture, Planning, and Consumer Culture on the American Front* (Minneapolis, MN, 2009). Robert Beauregard suggests that a certain ambivalence to city life manifested in the reluctance of state and federal regulation of the landscape and the lack of interest in developers to continue work in the urban core. Robert A. Beauregard, *When America Became Suburban* (Minneapolis, MN, 2006).

35 Joanne Spangler to Loewenstein, 9 March 1958, LAA.

36 Personal interview with Loewenstein homeowner, name withheld by request, 5 May 2010.

37 Undated speech notes for Woman's College by Loewenstein, LAA.

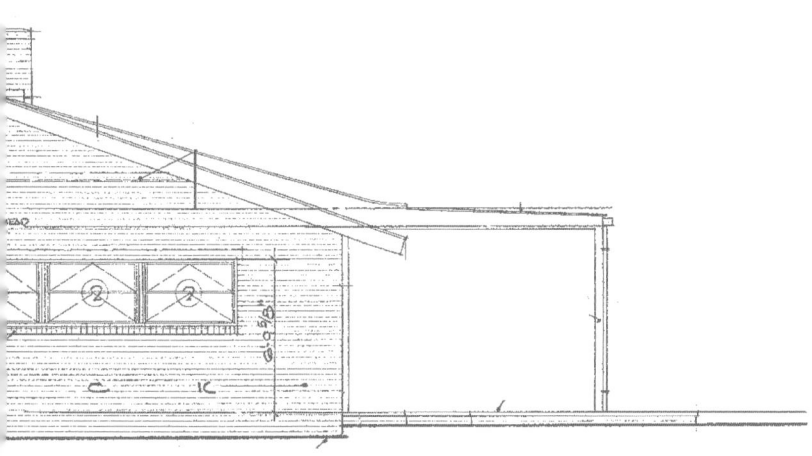

giving form to the dream house

Images by Marion Bertling from a photograph album documenting construction, 1952-1955. The building evolves from the site, workers add components throughout the construction process. (Private collection)

the tremendous housing boom of the twentieth century, particularly in the two decades following the end of World War II, wrought significant changes in cities and in family life throughout the United States. In all areas of the country, residents turned outward from the core to land at the edges of urban settlements, fashioning new ways of occupying the landscape in predominately horizontal houses on sprawling lots. The resultant neighborhoods and their attendant commercial areas provided a new structure for American communities and families largely based on gender roles, mobility, and compartmentalization in both class and race. Over a period of roughly twenty years, what people wanted in houses, how architects (and others) designed them, how designers furnished and modified them, how residents lived in them, and how homeowners paid for them all shifted dramatically in this suburban milieu.

The origins of these domestic transformations had begun much earlier. In the nineteenth century, Americans had wrestled with visions for appropriate housing forms and features to convey their sense of belonging, their aspirations of gentility, and their hopes for fitting in (and sometimes standing out) from others, just as those two or three generations on would do.[1] In the twentieth century, the automobile accelerated the scope of these changes and their location. Nearly every middle-class family owned at least one car,[2] and the automobile provided a quick and easy way to live further from the city center; some families were able to live their lives entirely apart from the ills perceived at the urban core.[3]

Much of what drove such a powerful transformation of domestic space and place related to the quest for the American dream of single-family homeownership. Many maintained an optimistic view, embedded in the collective consciousness of the nation before mid-century, that through suburban living, they could take a rightful place among peers as engaged democratic citizens in a great nation. Heady from victories of World War II, veterans returned home and turned their energy toward making houses that positioned them in a new place within social hierarchies. Just as the nation moved toward political, cultural, and social

leadership on the world stage, middle-class citizens assumed significantly new political and economic leverage as arbiters of shifting tastes and sensibilities regarding the American home.

DREAMING OF THE SINGLE FAMILY HOME

John Archer writes of a "dream house" ideal that permeated retail marketing, architectural design, media programming, and many other aspects of American culture at mid-century. The unfolding of this dream resulted in a raised awareness and changing expectations of what homeowners thought they should have in their houses. Families, young and old, having survived economic depression and two world wars, increasingly found themselves freed from the strictures of the Victorian world of their parents and grandparents. They aspired for economic and social freedom through status for themselves and their individual families. Sometimes without recognizing how asserting these personal visions would affect civic life and community vitality, they retreated to the suburbs and into the suburban residence.[4]

In the spreading one-story suburban homes, one encountered flexible public spaces. Representing social and physical mobility, these more fluid and conjoined living and dining spaces reflected shifts in the means and scale of entertaining at mid-century. Even the kitchens that supported this new lifestyle were sometimes open to the public spaces of the house. Outfitted with the latest appliances (electric ranges, dishwashers, trash compactors, and disposals), ideal kitchens quickly gained a reputation as places of deep efficiency, places that would liberate matriarchs from meal preparation and situate them more deeply into social practices in the open core of the house. The more efficient kitchen also meant that the hostess might need less help for food preparation and cleanup, directly affecting the decreasing presence of either live-in or day servants in the household.[5]

As the public areas solidified, families relocated their activities to a family or recreation room at the center of which often stood the suburban citizen's viewfinder to the world: the television. Around this altar to entertainment and communication, family members and visitors drew chairs, forming small communities unto themselves, isolated physically from their peers in both suburban and urban areas but connected deeply through the media form to tens of thousands of others tuned in to this societal lens. Some of what they saw there inevitably influenced the way they lived, the portal to the outside world serving both as a one-way screen on a consumer driven, automobile-fascinated, ever questing society and as its mirror.[6]

Private areas of the house stood beyond these public and semi-public spaces and provided not only resting places for family members but also storage spaces for the accumulation of consumer goods and the stuff of everyday life. Organized around central hallways that served as circulation paths, built-in closets and drawers lent easy access to storage and strictly defined the resultant architectural spaces beyond as bedrooms for family members. Situated amidst the built-ins, compartmentalized bathrooms — growing in abundance and complexity with the passage of time — allowed residents to dwell with comfort and sanitation options nearby. This confluence of storage, comfort, and sanitation insulated the bedrooms, making them solely occupied chambers rather than places of sharing as they had been in previous centuries.

Encasing the interior spaces — a matter of great debate among design practitioners, contractors, and increasingly, the public — required careful attention and regulation to stitch together

landscape and interior elements in a quest for spaciousness, no matter the size of the house.[7] Through picture windows, glass walls, open patios and decks, and other filters, residents of the home linked their domestic lives to an idealized sense of nature in the yard and lot beyond the house. Looking back at them, neighbors utilized similar filters to conform and stand out. One key shelter point, semi-enclosed and sometimes detached, the carport stood as a symbolic "home for the car," entwined with and embedded into the home for people. As another key link to the outside world, the automobile's presence in the suburban landscape — nestled into a berth astride the residence — represented mobility just as the public rooms did on the interior. These domestic assemblages in total, set along curving streets and on relatively large lots, bore the brand of freedom from social constraint from the urban collective, espousing a new vision for the city, one shaped by individual needs and wants far removed from community.

The landscaped lots, defined by wide manicured lawns and a variety of plantings, suggested a further link to individual values writ on the landscape. The lawn itself, symbol of the care and pride of the homeowner to keep it smooth and weed-free, spoke to the homogeneity of suburban culture, seemingly free from people different than the ideal.[8] The suburban infrastructure lent further credence to the anti-urban sentiments of suburban dwellers. Miles of paved streets, sewer and water lines, and electric service wires carried city services to these areas and represented tens of thousands of dollars of investments in local governments and utilities companies in the suburban neighborhood. Lack of public sidewalks cut down on street life and discouraged walks through the neighborhood. Cul-de-sac streets and gated subdivisions spoke the language of division and borders — looking inward rather than connecting outward.

Given this tabula rasa approach to the consumption of the landscape for suburban lots, one might expect new homeowners to embrace contemporary rather than traditional features for their homes. But time and again, they did the reverse, perhaps to fit in with their neighbors. By investing in a more conventional dwelling with Classical or Colonial Revival-style features — rather than an avant-garde house stripped of references to the past — owners ensured the longer-term stability of their financial investment by a perceived easier transference of the property when put up for sale. Moreover, by utilizing traditional design vocabulary for their dwellings, residents spoke the nearly homogeneous language of white, middle-class suburbia. In speaking other architectural languages or forms, designers and dwellers moved beyond the cultural and social norms into an elitist and artistic landscape, unconnected from the democratic ideals (and corresponding architectural forms and details) of the founding citizens of the nation. By building a modern dwelling, people spoke of difference and discord, not fitting in with others around them — an un-American approach to life. And yet, some suburban citizens did celebrate difference with Modern structures and landscapes.

A questioning of the status quo embodied in these dwellings indicates room in the suburban landscape for dissenters. They, too, sought a retreat from the busy life of the city about them, but the expression of that sentiment did not rely on the traditional symbolic elements of most structures. Designs promoted as stylistically fresh and efficient might have had more to do with the high cost of traditional forms and features compared to their modern counterparts, an idea with some application in the costly world of home ownership. With new lighting and window technology, as well as new systems technologies, designers, builders, and

owners could rely less on customary building practices. At mid-century, entire walls of glass, sliding doors, and air conditioning all made possible an opening of the traditional house form onto the landscape. Beyond the obvious opportunity to blend inside and outside, the reduction of design restrictions due to materiality and technology lessened, offering opportunities for more open houses with contemporary rather than traditional exteriors and interiors. Not just a question of surface treatment alone, Sandy Isenstadt observes that houses of the period, no matter the stylistic genre, responded to homeowner desires for a new sense of spaciousness, one in which Americans placed a premium on big houses with large rooms, fluid floor plans, and spreading lots.[9]

Much like design efforts for houses in the nineteenth and twentieth centuries, architects and builders of mid-century suburban residences devised three-part schemes for dividing space within suburban structures. In one area residents and visitors occupied main living and dining spaces, and sometimes a less formal family room — all spaces primarily dedicated to entertaining. Nearby, designers located rooms that comprised a work core (kitchen, laundry, and attendant storage) with proximate adjacencies. The third portion of the house provided the location for bedrooms, bathrooms, and clothing storage, private areas rarely on view to visitors.

The spreading one-story plans represented the key difference between earlier house forms in this tripartite scheme and dwellings of the mid-century. Because the size of residential building lots remained relatively large, builders, designers, and owners all saw the opportunity to unstack the traditional two story house with its central hall and stair, opening a plethora of configurations that relied less on strict symmetry and more on fluid relationships among the spaces. Along with open floor plans that residents desired and design professionals espoused, stretching buildings along the landscape gave greater freedom to the building envelope and expanded the notion of spaciousness on the interior as well as signifying breadth from the exterior view. An expansive lawn with carefully manicured plantings accentuated the perception of spaciousness from the streets and from neighboring lots and homeowners.

Despite the relative freedom of the building envelope, increasingly standardized building materials provided order and coherence to compositions and, importantly, kept the price of construction affordable. As owners sought low-profile roofs, designers specified them, and builders constructed them — minimizing traditional attics and dramatically reducing the amount of material and the cost of construction. Omitting basements, too, lessened the financial commitment for a suburban dwelling, these design decisions necessitating the provision for storage *within* rather than above or below the living spaces.

With vast expanses of glazing and utilizing natural materials, architects, designers, and owners opened living spaces into the suburban landscape, inviting the outside in and bringing nature and its influences into the scheme — and into contact with humans. Modern dwellings, particularly, relied on the large glass windows, walls, and sliding doors to provide color, texture, and visual interest in rooms stripped of traditional décor and finishes. Designers of the mid-century generally mixed furniture styles rather than specifying the purity and singularity of a single style. This approach, with space for inherited furniture alongside mid-century modern furnishings, suggested a means for dwellers to embrace both past and present in their near environment. Importantly, by including built-in cabinets and closets, designers

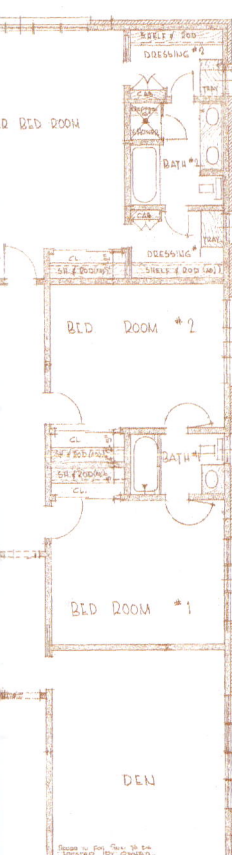

lessened the need for storage pieces, particularly in the private zones of the residence. Corresponding to a standardization in building materials, furniture manufacturers also standardized sizes of furniture and accessories as mass-produced items flowed from department stores into interiors of mid-century dwellings, much as they had in the previous century.

Even though homeowners had a wide variety of choices, designers simplified wall coverings and textiles to coordinate seamless interiors and embrace a new vision for design. They reduced clutter in decorative accessories, building on a general trend toward clean and simple living after the end of the world war. Ironically, the 1950s also saw an explosion in both the quantity and availability of consumer goods.[10] In the end, acquisition of goods won out over their reduction and removal, bringing the consumer society of the latter half of the twentieth century into clear view.[11]

Many of these changes stem from mediated ideas of house in magazines, in newspapers, on television, and on the landscape.[12] Design magazines, in particular, provided floor plans to copy, sometimes with designers adapting owner-directed amendment. These magazines also contained a great abundance of advertisements for the latest building materials and technologies. The advertisements for furnishings, equipment, and finishes showed a growing industry centered on the construction of the single-family home. From trade journals for architects and designers to magazines geared to the average American housewife, one could view a plethora of design choices from modern to traditional and every hybridized form between. Despite the presence, though, of modern stylistic choices in the professional periodicals, most publications incorporated traditional suburban residences rather than their contemporary counterparts. In the mass media, modern dwellings appeared, if at all, as more unusual offerings, clearly distinct from the mainstream.[13]

In communities across the United States, profiles on homeowners, architects, and designers unfolded in daily or weekly newspapers, which young men on bicycles carried into the suburbs. The "home" section of these publications contained visual images, descriptions, and design philosophies for new homes. For thousands of readers, they served as guides for keeping up with one's neighbors in a race to be characterized as homeowners of good taste.

Television provided another visual source for ideas of the home, though it was a media space where traditional buildings outweighed their modern counterparts. In the 1950s and 1960s, one only had to turn on the television to enter the Nelson's traditionally styled Sycamore Road residence with its Colonial style furnishings (*The Adventures of Ozzie and Harriet*, 1952–1966). Next door, at least on the airwaves, the Andersons took up life on *Father Knows Best,* (1954–1958) in a similar traditional home. Along with the Cleavers (*Leave It to Beaver*, 1957–1963) and the Stones (*The Donna Reed Show*, 1958–1966), the "average" white suburban family lived in Colonial Revival — style dwellings outfitted with traditional furniture. One had to look to nontraditional families — those at first without children (*I Love Lucy*, 1951–1957) or as a divorcee (*Life with Lucy*, 1962–1968), with uncles as the patriarchal head of household (*Family Affair*, 1966–1971), or couples on an implied second marriage and lifestyle change (*Green Acres*, 1965–1971) to see glints of Modernism, often in an urban setting.

A flip of the channel brought the viewer back to the safety of more middle-of-the-road designed spaces, away from their modern counterparts on *My Three Sons* (1960–1972) and its two homes for the Douglas family, *Petticoat Junction* (1963–1970) and its more rural homeplace, and to the palace of a house for the Clampetts in *The Beverly Hillbillies* (1962–1971). In all these shows, the traditional won out as visual rhetoric over the modern. It was only with the co-mingled family of Mike and Carol Brady that the modern house, designed by one of the lead characters as architect, offered an idealized suburban space for *The Brady Bunch* (1969–1974).

The suburban neighborhood on the small screen thus stood as a decidedly conservative place, stylistically if not philosophically. The accoutrements of suburban family life served as an expression of television producers' and production staff's idealized views of the suburban world, at the center of which stood the single-family home. These domestic spaces remained the safe haven for the protection of family values even alongside the actual suburbs — restrictive places devoid of racial, class, and gender complications later understood to rest beneath the managed images of mid-century family life. As television viewers consumed these places and made choices of their own to shape their suburban lives, undoubtedly the world of media influenced the physical one.

From printed sources and from television shows, and from the existing housing stock in suburbs throughout the nation, residents of the suburbs could find plenty of guides to amenities and good taste. As Russell Lynes, long-time editor of *Harper's Magazine*, suggested satirically and vaguely, "the only thing that is more to be guarded against than bad taste is good taste."[14] Thus within a framework of broadly accepted canons of design, the individual interpreted through the single-family freestanding dwelling a wide array of stylistic, material, and furnishings choices possible in a new world of personal choice, fabricating a suburban world that combined both independence and social control. In other words, others tolerated individual expression within narrowly defined stylistic and design boundaries — one could be avant-garde, but only slightly so, in order not to offend one's neighbors and the sense of the community in aesthetic matters.

DWELLING IN BETWEEN

The Modern house, on an open lot with its fluid layout and eclectic furnishings schemes represented a nightmare for many but a dream for some. It suggested an alternative to suburban ranch houses that used a well-defined lexicon — traditional room layouts furnished with period reproductions in closed, paneled rooms surmounted with elaborate trim, casings, and decorative wallpaper. By using Classical- and Colonial-Revival-style details and features in these ranch houses, architects, designers, builders, and owners tethered their visions of themselves to political and social leaders of the past — elite white men carrying out the American colonial experience. Modern structures swept aside this architectural rhetoric. Yet the designers, builders, and owners of Modern houses forecast a no less stable world; only this world borrowed on contemporary understandings of materials, spaces, and issues — they were houses "of the age."

A house in between — the dream, the reality, for many building at mid-century — suggested either a structure perhaps with an open plan but a traditional exterior shell or a house with a somber front facing the public thoroughfare but with expansive, fluid spaces at its rear, enclosed with glass to maximize the connection to the outdoors. In either scenario, the hybridization of architecture, interior design, furniture, and finishes represented the uncertainty of fitting in with or standing out from one's neighbors. Often more easily or readily changed, house interiors and furnishings were an ephemeral way for homeowners to modify their near environment and thus their identity. The landscape of buildings also could be readily modified, providing a truly outward sign to all passersby about values and identities of the residents. Sitting between these two ever-changing zones in the human environment, the building's more steady physicality and the relative high expense of alteration suggested the semi-permanence of the structure, one mediating between old and new, past and present, inside and out, in a conversation about values expressed within the "dream house" of the mid-century.

Largely in Greensboro, Edward Loewenstein experimented across houses of all three genre and influence, from traditional to Modern, with some houses in between. The first of the structures he designed in private practice on his own. As the work increased in the community, and as the firm formed, Loewenstein and his partner, Robert A. Atkinson Jr., took on junior designers and draftsmen who helped carry out the design intentions of the firm. He also worked with interior designers, lighting designers, and contractors who furthered the vision of Modern architecture, traditional dwelling, and houses between. In looking at Loewenstein's design work in this way, one understands the many decisions, equally reflective of client and architect, which shape the residences. Ultimately connected to a larger discourse about experimentation in design in the decades following the World War II, Loewenstein's brand of Modernism bears the marks of a second generation of young architects and designers, echoing and reinterpreting the work of their mentors — European and American designers and architects practicing in Modern ways.

PROTOTYPE : ARCHETYPE : HYBRID

In these first four houses, readers can see this intertwined and ever evolving design world and recognize connections with the broader practice of architecture and suburban life sounding and resounding in communities throughout the United States. Here we have the story of one architect who, having moved to a Southern community, brought a different way of seeing and thinking about design. For some of the houses, he and clients together pushed the sense of design thinking beyond mid-century norms. In other dwellings, clients resided happily, as had their forebears, in more traditionally styled rooms with period antiques and reproductions linking to the Colonial American experience. As the stories of these five houses unfold, we see the beginnings of design conversations that lasted throughout Loewenstein's career and were borne in the dwellings he realized over a twenty-year time span. By listening to the conversations, as translated in the buildings themselves, we hear a story of fluid understanding among styles, rather than the series of single-minded approaches so often equated with Modernism. With these stories, we also hear the voices of Loewenstein and his clients as they determined the best ways for themselves and their families to live at mid-century, linking to the practice of making home. Finally, we also hear the stories of dissent — particularly in the Modern homes — where clients and designers together shaped a different way of thinking that symbolized the cultural shifts of the 1950s and 1960s — the same shifts that ultimately brought four men to the Woolworth's counter in downtown Greensboro.

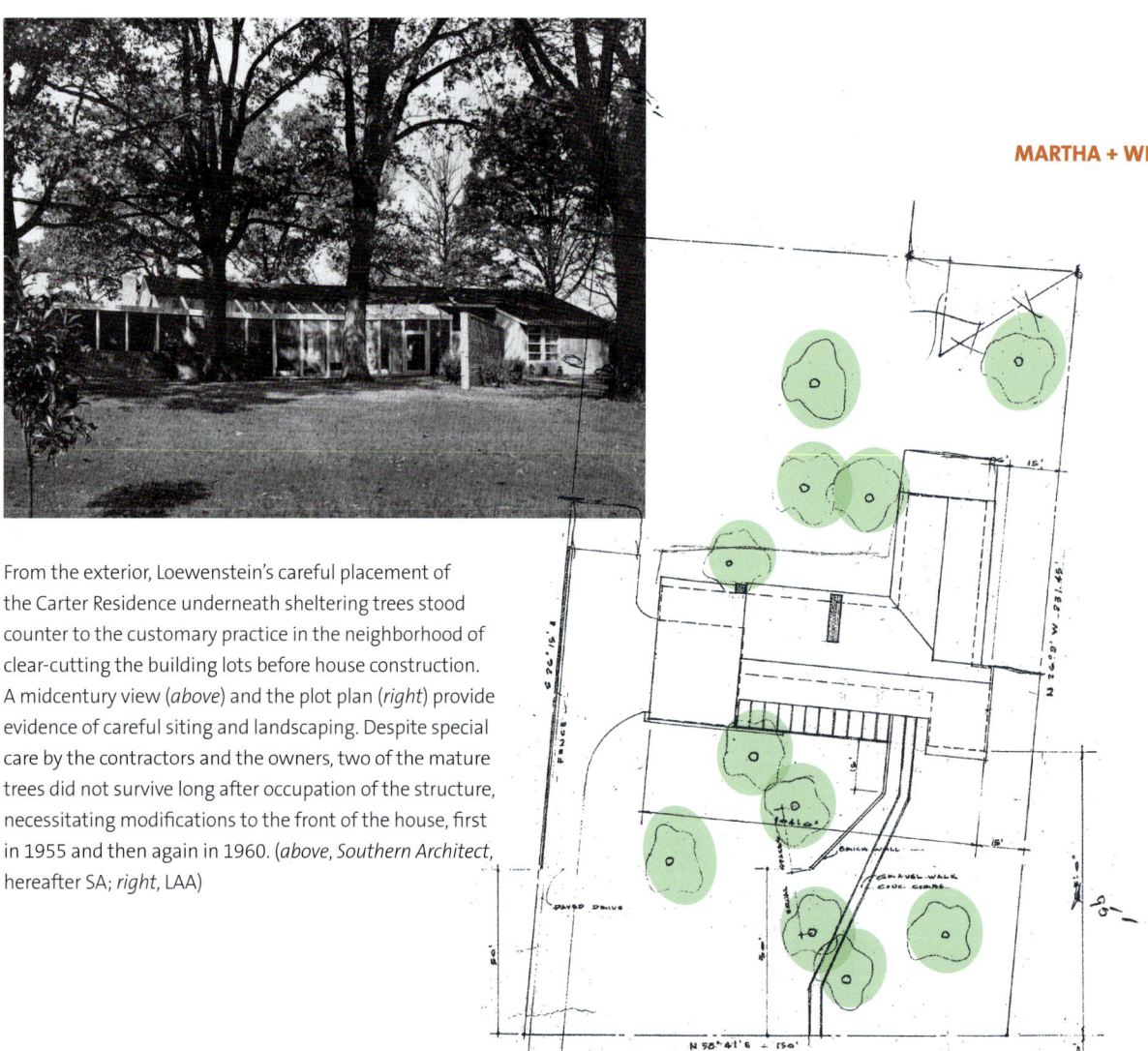

MARTHA + WILBUR L. CARTER, JR. RESIDENCE : GREENSBORO (1950–1951)

Though Loewenstein had been practicing in Greensboro since 1946 and had already designed more than a dozen residences, many acknowledge his first major Modern residential commission as the Carter Residence precisely at mid-century.[15] Highly visible within the Irving Park neighborhood, and on land purchased from Martha and Ceasar Cone, the visual impact of the Carter Residence at a prominent location certainly gave the community a fine example of the type of Modern dwelling emerging from the drawing boards of architects practicing after World War II. Built among traditional dwellings of two stories in the earlier-developed streetcar suburb of Irving Park, the house stuck out boldly. Nevertheless, Loewenstein's Modernist dwelling slipped onto the architectural landscape in a low-key manner, at least in the press accounts. A reporter for the *Greensboro Record* described it simply as "gracious, comfortable, and young" and recounted some of the details of the construction and design of the house related to the radiant floor heating, not mentioning the departure from more traditional vocabulary customary in the city's suburbs.

Loewenstein recognized the design importance of his first Modern structure and, in 1952, directed architectural photographer Joseph W. Molitor (New York) to make images of the Carter Residence along with the Bessemer Improvement Company Building, and Southeastern Radio Supply Building for firm marketing materials; all three buildings continued to be featured as important commissions in subsequent firm materials.[16] The house also appeared in *Southern Architect*, the North Carolina American Institute of Architect's Chapter publication, when it was recognized with a 1955 Merit Award.[17] In the national press, the editors of *Architectural Record* included the house in the November 1952 issue with additional photographs, a floor plan, and a story about the design process for the work.

From the exterior, Loewenstein's careful placement of the Carter Residence underneath sheltering trees stood counter to the customary practice in the neighborhood of clear-cutting the building lots before house construction. A midcentury view (*above*) and the plot plan (*right*) provide evidence of careful siting and landscaping. Despite special care by the contractors and the owners, two of the mature trees did not survive long after occupation of the structure, necessitating modifications to the front of the house, first in 1955 and then again in 1960. (*above*, *Southern Architect*, hereafter SA; *right*, LAA)

prototype

The Carters faced the same decision as many others building a "dream house" after the end of World War II: should they link to the traditional past or cast it aside for a more modern vision of what a house could look like? *Architectural Record* reporters indicated indecision on the clients' response to this question. Supported by the surviving correspondence in the firm archives and an oral history interview, Loewenstein developed two schemes for his clients, one based on a long horizontal, gable-roofed structure depicted in a copy by an unknown artist of Georgia O'Keeffe's *White Barn II* (1932), a painting in the Carters' art collection. In an alternative scheme for the house, in preliminary sketch form, Loewenstein articulated a two-story Georgian Revival dwelling, more in keeping with the other structures in Irving Park. When faced with the decision between the two, the Carters elected the Modern scheme based on cost and for the love of the open plan, and for the connection to the art work that served as inspiration for the architect. Loewenstein later wrote Florence A. Van Wyck, associate editor of *Architectural Record*, and explained:

> We started working with the Carters on an extremely contemporary house. Early in the design stage they visited a completed contemporary house which had been designed by its owner (not an architect) and they became very discouraged about modern architecture. We were requested to stop any more work until they could get a price or an estimated price on our preliminary drawings. A local contractor estimated the house and they decided they would rather have a traditional Georgian house. We completed drawings on this, through the working drawing stage and obtained an even more outrageous estimate. By the time all parties were numb on the subject and the Carters decided to let us carry the project through as a contemporary project. As it progressed, their parents, who were very conservative, had become very enthusiastic about it and we have received violent comments in both directions from neighbors and friends.[18]

Fifty years later, Wilbur Carter proudly tells the story of the painting, still in his possession, and its impact on the design of the well-loved house that he and his wife built and lived in for five decades.[19]

With Modern art as the design inspiration for the dwelling, Loewenstein included in prototypical form nearly all of the ideas that matured in his residential Modern work over two decades, ideas that distinguished his work in the more humanist or warm strain of Modernism. Thus the Carter "dream house" stood, like others of its ilk across the United States, as an expression of cultural values. In the house, this family espoused a new design vision for American home life that spoke of new relationships among family members, servants, and visitors. They traded the formal, hierarchical relationships of more traditional styles and forms for more fluid interrelationships among the people and the various spaces within the building, and they did so in a manner that, at least according to one printed source, remained true to a sense of Southern graciousness. With this house, then, the Carters and Loewenstein (along with interior decorator Blair Smith and builders from the Brooks Lumber Company) all spoke in a dialect that diverged from Southern mores.

For this commission, Loewenstein first experimented with separation of **public and private** spaces in the overall organizational scheme. He also worked to connect **indoors and outdoors**, first at the Carter house and then through his residential buildings. Here and elsewhere, he hid the **front entrance** from obvious view. He included **built-in storage** to reduce the amount of furniture needed and to divide space. He embraced sophisticated, multivalent strategies for natural and electric **lighting** in this dwelling and expanded this experimentation in future homes. Finally, he adopted a palette of **materials** centered in North Carolina building traditions to soften the Modern structures in their immediate context. Loewenstein explained by letter:

> Materials have been chosen first from the standpoint of texture and color, and then durability, ease of maintenance, and adaptability. We like the flagstone and Vinyl-cork floors, the glass porch roof and the general layout. We are delighted with the use of wormy chestnut and so are a rare species of bugs, which is attempting to inhabit the worm holes. In the next application of stain to the exterior finish, we expect to add a bug inhibitor to eliminate this condition.[20]

All of these ideas Loewenstein introduced at the Carter Residence influenced future commissions, either at his own hand or with the assistance of the various firm employees in the production of Modernist dwellings.

As originally designed by Loewenstein, the front entry sequence for visitors included negotiating an 8-foot-high brick wall, passing by the solar room toward a single-leaf door. Standing at the intersection between the public and private wings of the house, the front entry offered the visitor a moment of orientation. To the left, the visitor saw across an expansive vista, with light sweeping in from the solar room at the front of the house to the window wall view at the north end of the living room toward the

For the Carter Residence, Loewenstein designed an L-shaped plan with a public wing parallel to the road and a perpendicular wing of bedrooms. The landscape captured in the ell at the rear provides ample space for a large patio for outdoor living and protected the back yard from street traffic. A carport occupied the left end of the structure and provided a covered space for automobiles; it also sheltered the service entrance and wing to the house. The service end of the public block of the house, parallel to the street, included the carport, a maid's room, a laundry room, and storage cabinets. By zoning this end of the house for service, Loewenstein left open the plan of spaces in the public wing. In the private side of the house, perpendicular from the street and the front entrance, the architect clustered closets and storage systems, as well as bathrooms, to provide visual and auditory separation from one bedroom to the next. Loewenstein designed a wide hallway on the west side of this wing, supplying valuable space for other living activities for family members, with direct visual and physical access to the backyard beyond. (LAA)

As drawn, the entry point to the structure took tangible form as a hidden (or less than obvious) entrance. (LAA)

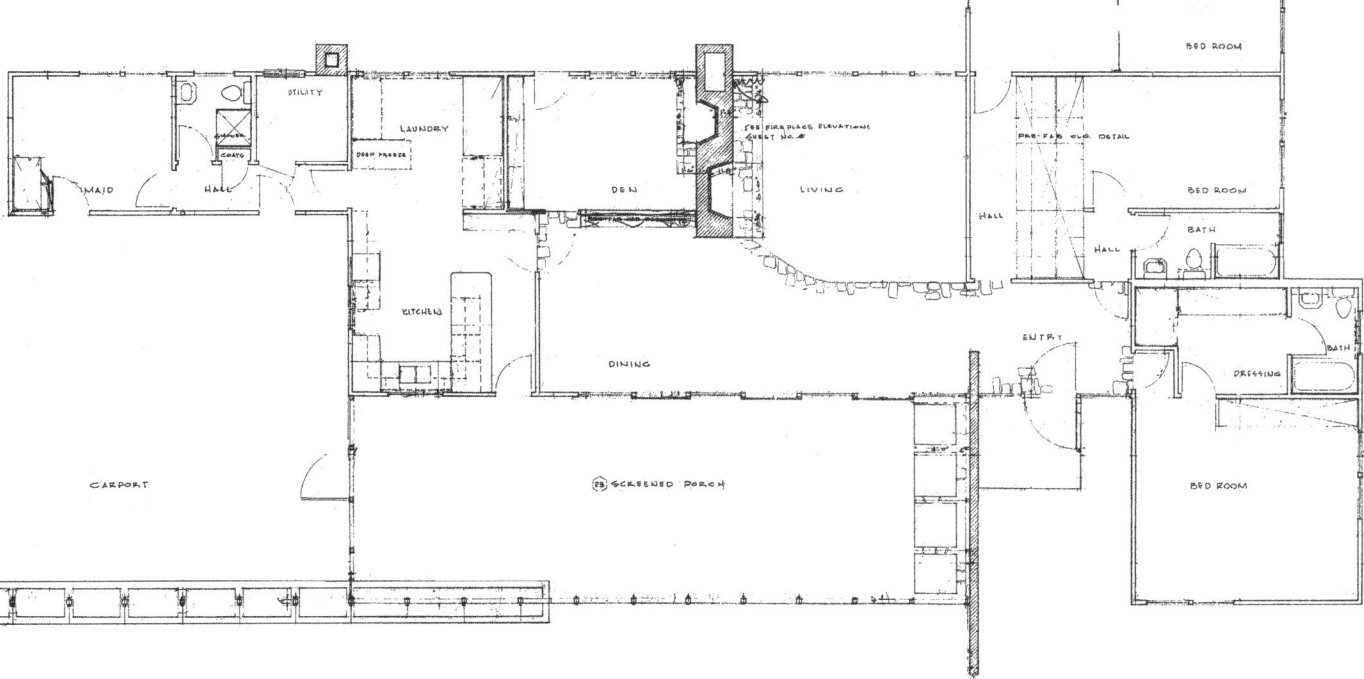

The mid-century view above depicts the hous shortly after construction. Within two decade of construction, the owners removed the bric wall (to the left) along with making changes t the solar cell room. (SA)

backyard. By contrast, the vista toward the bedroom wing, blocked by solid walls and a series of doors, indicated that this portion of the house contained family quarters, not easily accessed visually or physically by those outside the family.

Built-in cabinets and closets abounded in the private wing of the house, and in the service section of the public wing — a design feature expanded dramatically in future Loewenstein commissions. Through their introduction, Loewenstein minimized the need for significant furnishings in bedrooms and related spaces. Consolidating the storage systems in the kitchen and working areas of the home allowed servants to intertwine within the life of the home. Live-in quarters for hired help spoke to the socioeconomic status of the owners, though their mere presence encapsulates one of the inherent tensions in mid-century life: the mixing of race and class within the single family home.

Though Loewenstein and his lighting consultants developed more sophisticated lighting schemes in houses built after the Carter Residence, in this building, the manipulation of natural light shows the experience he intended for the residents and visitors. Light flooded from the south façade into the solar room and then more deeply into the living and dining rooms beyond. Particularly in the winter months, this lighting strategy had implication for a passive solar heating of the bluestone floor, allowing homeowners to harness energy and reduce utility bills. The architect designed the open façade on the north side of the house and the one on the west side of the bedroom wing to link living spaces and the yard and views beyond. These fenestrations also allowed light to sweep in, though not as dramatically, as an even wash throughout the year. With the service aspects of the building on the west, and the bedroom wing on the east, Loewenstein minimized fenestration on these façades.

In the original scheme for the structure, Loewenstein envisioned a natural materials palette with wormy chestnut

Over the two phases of construction, the owners enclosed the screened porch with a glass wall, removed the glass roof and replaced it with roof decking to match the remainder of the low-pitched roof, and shortened the slightly curving entrance wall, originally designed to provide some visual separation for the solar room on the front of the house from the street. (C. Timothy Barkley Photography, hereafter CTB)

vertical siding, bluestone floors, wood floors, and rose-colored brick walls. Deployed both inside and outside of the structure, these materials smoothed the transition between outdoors and the interior, just as the clients had desired. Working with Loewenstein on the project was interior decorator Blair Smith, later employed at the Loewenstein-Atkinson firm. Together, architect and designer developed a colorful furnishings scheme, reported in the *Greensboro Daily News*, to contrast with the natural palette in the architectural enclosure.

For the Carter Residence, Loewenstein designed highly colorful tile bathrooms, as well as bathroom fittings (medicine cabinets, built-in toothbrush holders, toilet paper holders, and more) and hardware regularly included in the later houses. Thus colored furnishings and finishes on the interior contrasted with the natural palette of materials specified for the architectural enclosure, unifying the exterior and interior appearance.

Overhanging eaves provide a sharp shadow line and emphasize the horizontality of the building in the landscape at the carport (*above left*), along the bedroom wing (*above middle*) and even within the interior, with its horizontal sliding glass doors set within a track (*above right*). Where neighboring buildings conquered by height and external decoration, Loewenstein's Modern structures settled horizontally into Irving Park. Rather than stacking stories (as would be the case in more traditional residential forms), Loewenstein spread buildings across the landscape, taking advantage of views and site features, preserving mature trees, and linking outside to inside in sophisticated relationships throughout each scheme. (Patrck Lee Lucas, hereafter PLL)

Loewenstein provided for a solar room on the front of this remarkable open, one-story horizontal plan, and sensitively nestled the house among a grove of mature trees already on the lot. He separated this space from the adjoining living room and dining room through a series of large sliding glass doors. Typical of Loewenstein's designs, the screened room doubled the living space during temperate seasons of the year. Later enclosed with glass walls, the year-round space manifested a Loewenstein design strategy for double living spaces, often stacked side by side in the plan to give perceptions of spaciousness, fluidity, and flexibility in room use and furnishings. A mid-century view (*above far right*) of the solar room contrasts with the current-day view (*right*) to demonstrate changes made to this space over several decades: enclosing part of the glass ceiling and replacing screen panels with glass. (*above far right*, SA; *right*, CTB)

Loewenstein placed a 15' x 50' "solar cell" room on the south side of the structure (*above*), originally designed as a screened porch, to capture southeasterly breezes and bring them to the adjoining living and dining rooms. In winter, the native bluestone floor absorbed heat during the day and radiated it out over the evening hours; in summer, eaves and the mature trees (for a short time) shielded the interior from the sun. The view framed to the front lawn links interior to exterior through a glass wall between the living/dining rooms and the solar room. The open beams of the solar room space echo use of the gable space within later houses. Loewenstein often paired these full-height spaces with clerestory windows in irregular polygonal shapes. (CTB)

Simultaneous to the Carter commission, Loewenstein designed the **A. M. Fleischmann Residence in Fayetteville, North Carolina in 1951**, as well as the **Ann and Lloyd P. Tate Residence in Pinehurst, North Carolina in 1952**. In both of these structures, Loewenstein experimented with the same palettes of materials and details as seen in the Carter Residence. In the Fleischmann Residence, Loewenstein continued to test his theories of Modernism, elaborating the L-shaped plan of the Carter Residence and including a large screened room at the rear — rather than the front of the home. In the bedroom wing, Loewenstein borrows from lessons learned in the Carter Residence by incorporating a generously wide hallway doubling both as a circulation link and an activity space. With the Tate Residence, however, Loewenstein pushes the boundaries of warm Modernism toward the more severe Modernism of his contemporaries on faculty in the North Carolina State University School of Design. This most Modern of all dwellings, like a number of Loewenstein commissions, resulted from conversations with clients and a choice between Modern and traditional versions of the same plan. The Fleischman Residence (*top*) and the Tate Residence (*bottom*) show more Modern characteristics than their counterparts in Greensboro. (*top*, PLL; *bottom*, Private collection)

35

ELEANOR + MARION BERTLING RESIDENCE : GREENSBORO (1953)

About a mile from the Carter Residence, Loewenstein worked to develop a more compact house with further experimentation in design approaches and details as a prototype for his Modern designs. As he elaborated this Modernist lexicon, he brought these design features and processes to greater resolution in the Bertling Residence — and in his own residence of 1954 — as well as houses of the latter 1950s located throughout the community. Like the Carter Residence before it, the Bertling's house slipped onto the scene with little notice in the local press, despite the opportunity for notoriety because of its difference. In welcoming the Bertlings to the street, nearly three-dozen nearby residents signed a petition of support in the construction of a Modernist dwelling, flying in the face of the unwritten restrictions from the planning and zoning department to prohibit Modern structures in the Kirkwood neighborhood. It seemed that a Modern dwelling that maintained a large distance from the street and a low profile on the landscape could enter a traditional neighborhood, as long as it did so gently. In defying the development guidelines for the neighborhood, the Bertlings and Loewenstein indicated a different social order for at least part of the community based on Modernism as well as an embrace of the automobile as design inspiration.

In thinking about the car as a prominent and visible part of the residence, as opposed to a feature hidden, Loewenstein celebrated the presence of the twentieth-century form of transportation in his architecture. Loewenstein made it clear where the automobile penetrated the building at the point closest to the street, emphasizing the garage over the pedestrian entrance to the building for visitors. The entry sequence resulted in a crossroads in plan, with a guest room to the south of the entry, the living room to the east, dining room to the west, and bedroom wing to the north. The architect thus provided a point of orientation and clarity in organization for visitor and family member alike, zoning the house into public and private areas, a division readily supported by use and function.

Unlike the Carter Residence, the Bertling Residence, entirely surrounded by trees on a wooded site, offered additional privacy and a further merging of building and landscape, underscored by a handsome soft-pink brick exterior and the presence of a large screen porch at the rear. From the street, the Bertlings' house slipped quietly across the landscape, a horizontal underscoring of the wooded site. Loewenstein introduced openings on façades other than the front elevation, leaving passersby to speculate about the closed nature of the house from its exterior appearance. (PLL)

The wooded lot obscures the presence of the house in the streetscape. The garage sits forward of the main mass of the building, further distancing and sheltering the home from the road and to passersby. A circular driveway passes through the garage with openings on both the front façade and the service yard side of the dwelling, enabling the client to pass through the structure. Oral tradition indicated that the client requested this double-sided garage because, as a doctor, he frequently received requests for services in the dark of the night and did not wish to back a car out from a garage. (*left*, Private collection; *right*, PLL)

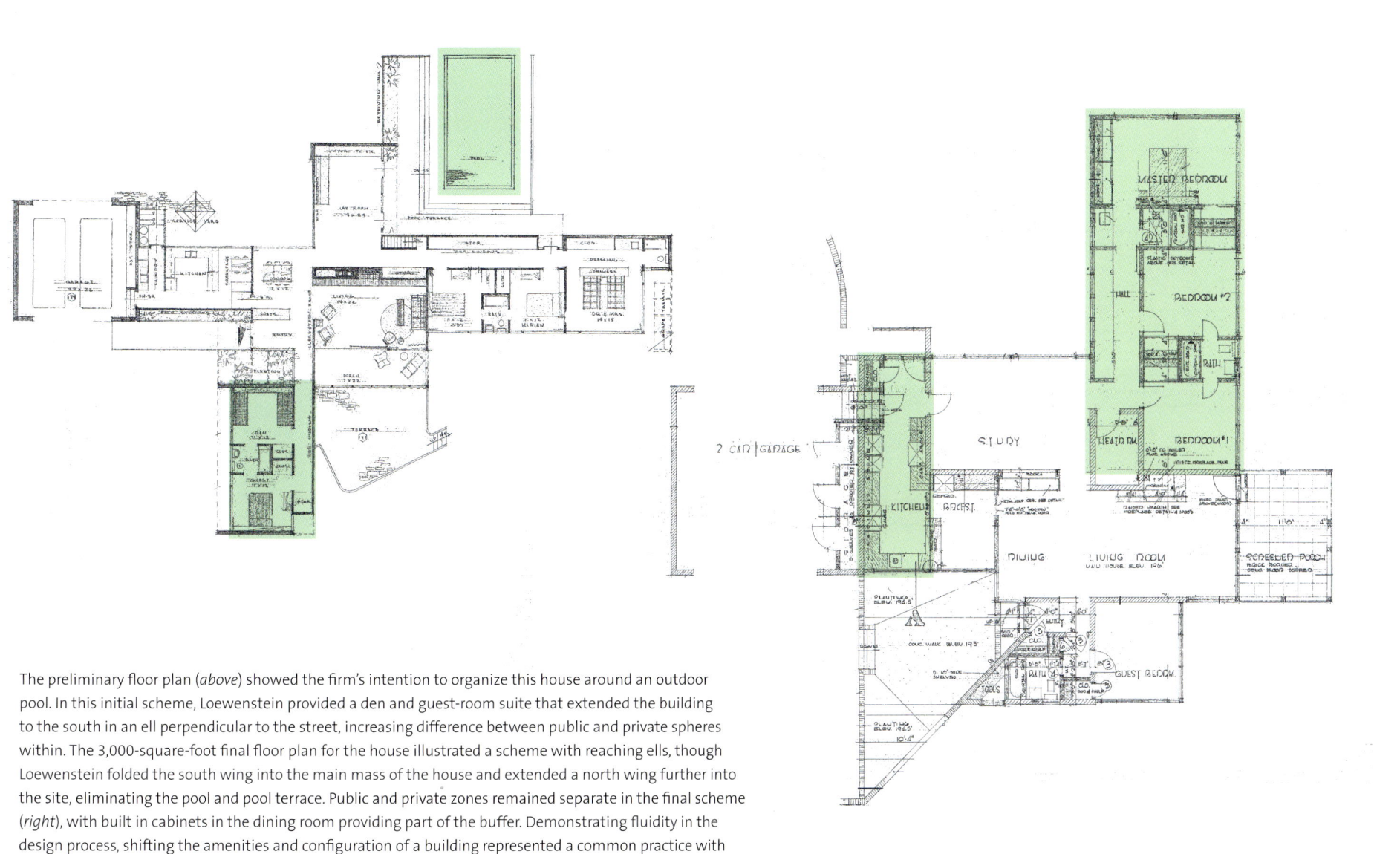

The preliminary floor plan (*above*) showed the firm's intention to organize this house around an outdoor pool. In this initial scheme, Loewenstein provided a den and guest-room suite that extended the building to the south in an ell perpendicular to the street, increasing difference between public and private spheres within. The 3,000-square-foot final floor plan for the house illustrated a scheme with reaching ells, though Loewenstein folded the south wing into the main mass of the house and extended a north wing further into the site, eliminating the pool and pool terrace. Public and private zones remained separate in the final scheme (*right*), with built in cabinets in the dining room providing part of the buffer. Demonstrating fluidity in the design process, shifting the amenities and configuration of a building represented a common practice with the Loewenstein-Atkinson firm. Loewenstein and firm employees bring simplicity and coherency to the plan, working through design development to the floor plan as built. (LAA)

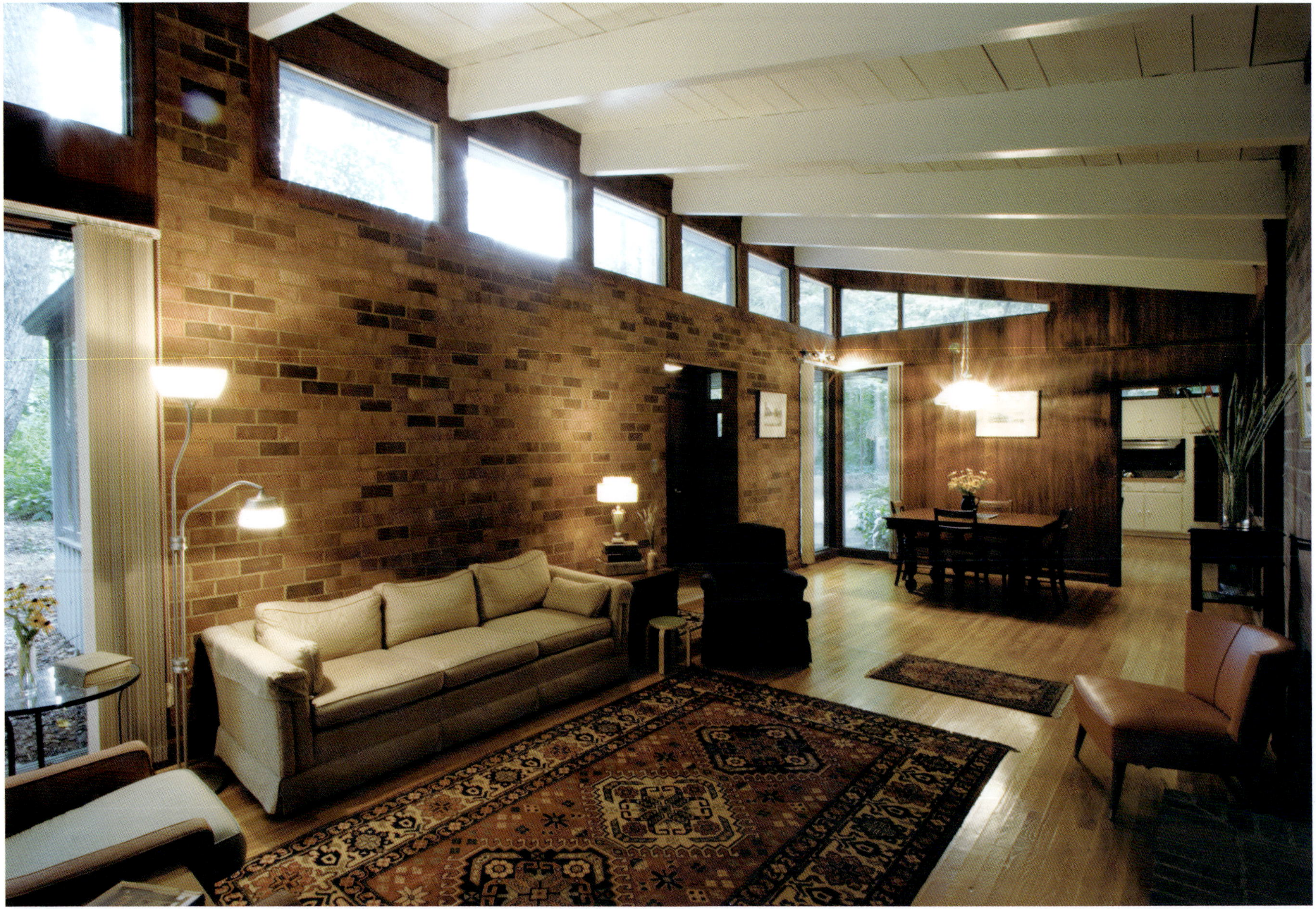

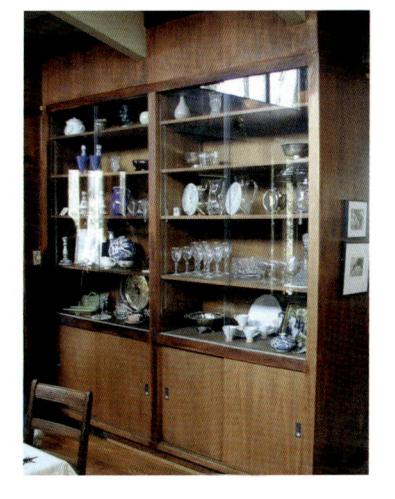

South-facing clerestory windows allowed light to sweep into the living and dining room spaces, supplementing the window wall at the east end of the room (*left*), bringing a sense of warmth and dynamism to these Modernist interiors. In the bedroom wing, Loewenstein placed east-facing windows to capture morning light. Loewenstein softened the impact of this same light on the living room with the screened porch to the east. High windows in the kitchen and dining room allowed residents to view visitors to the house along the entry sequence. Other special lighting effects, so much a part of the sophisticated schemes in the later structures, were not employed in the Bertling Residence. (CTB)

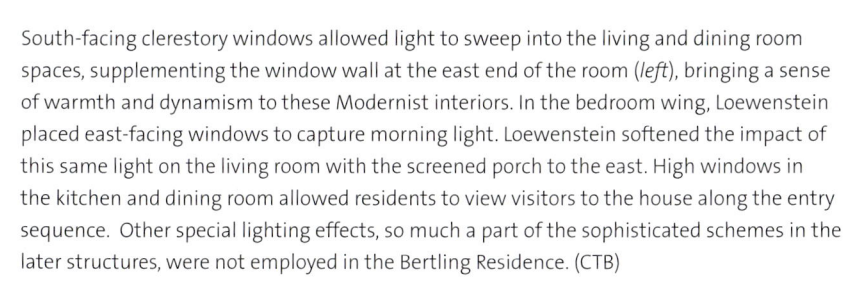

Realizing the melding of both exterior and interior experience into a seamless opportunity of interactivity, Loewenstein continued the explorations of the Carter Residence in this smaller structure. Echoing earlier efforts, he exposed beams in the ceilings of the public rooms to give a sense of openness. He picked up the theme of open rooms, eliminating flat roofs on the interior of the public areas in the structure. He connected inside to outside with a screened porch that opened off the living room. With well-placed windows on three of the elevations, Loewenstein captured landscape views, bringing fluidity to interior-exterior divisions. He enlivened and enriched the interior experience through a matching materials palette both outside and in. By introducing window fenestrations of various shapes and configurations, Loewenstein further energized the scheme and provided important views for the clients, linking the outside to the interior. (CTB)

A massive built-in cabinet that fills one entire wall of the dining room and provides a colorful, glass-fronted storage system for china and a divider for the more private family room behind it. This centrally located built-in within the scheme appears in later Loewenstein structures as a key focal point and space-saving room divider and storage system. In the private areas and the service sector of the home, Loewenstein incorporated built-in storage to isolate the bedroom wing and in compartmentalizing the bath and storage functions attendant in that area. For service, storage helped provide a sound barrier between garage and kitchen, a theme drawn on by the firm in the following two decades. (PLL)

Corrugated fiberglass sheeting on the roof of the screened porch helped weave new materials and technologies into the scheme alongside more traditional materials (*above left*). The translucent roof permitted light to penetrate the depth of the screened porch into the large glass wall of the living room to the west. The interior featured the same gently salmon-hued brick as a means to carry the outside in. The richly hued walnut paneling supplemented the warmth of the pink-toned brick and the honey-colored wood floor, all tying the building to the natural environment. By contrast, three distinct, brightly colored tile bathrooms showed the ingenuity of the Loewenstein office, and provided a punctuation to the otherwise natural palette of materials for the structure (*above right*). Providing the latest in cabinetry, in each bathroom a beveled sink mirror raised vertically from sink to ceiling to reveal the shelves behind. Balancing innovation and natural materials, Loewenstein softened the Modernist palette of materials in this and later homes. (PLL)

archetype

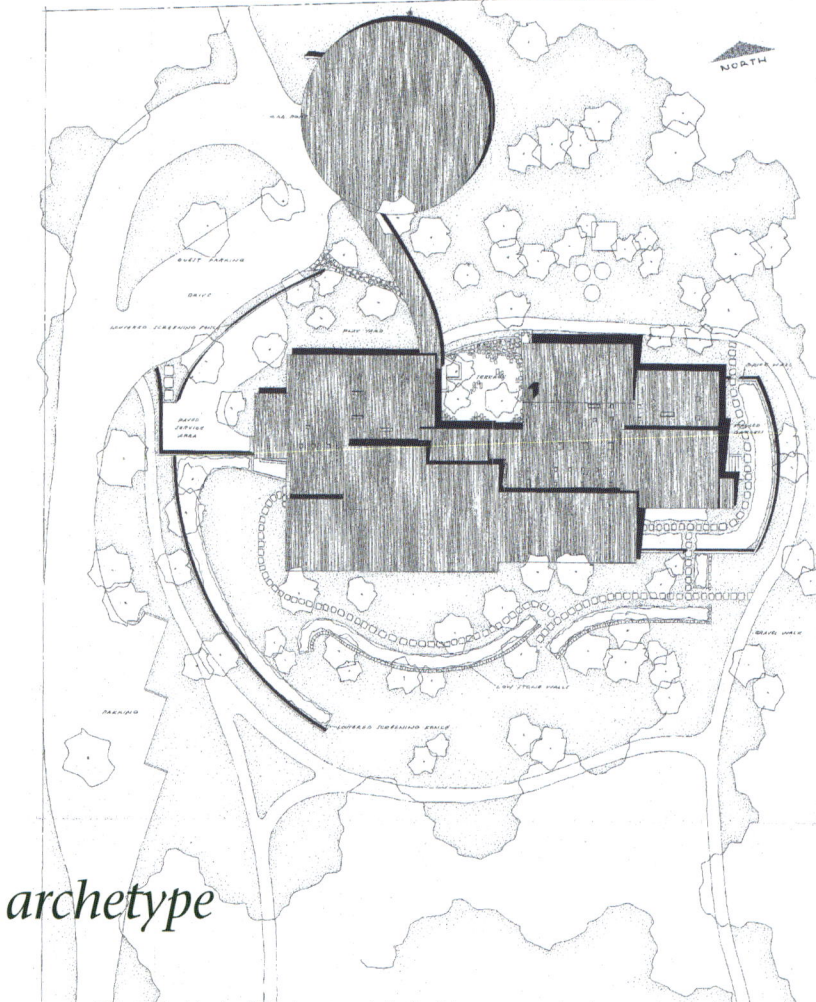

The main block of the Loewenstein Residence, organized around an entry court, opens to a walkway and the circular carport beyond. Loewenstein carefully placed overlapping, rectilinear roof planes to layer the composition. The house sits at the back third of the lot, distant from the road. The viewer approaches the house from the south façade, viewing the structure through a wooded lot. (LAA)

FRANCES + EDWARD LOEWENSTEIN RESIDENCE : GREENSBORO (1954)

So many of the experiments with space perception and use, storage, lighting, materials, and design philosophies took a more revolutionary form in Loewenstein's own house. Ostensibly designed to specifically suit Modernist sensibilities, Loewenstein also accounted for his wife's more eclectic tastes in the interiors, furnishings, and finishes. Further, as the house took form, Loewenstein's professional world changed in the establishment of a partnership. He took on partners and employees and began to direct their design approaches rather than undertaking the majority of the work himself. In addition, the design team for this structure increased beyond the borders of the firm to include New York designer Sarah Hunter Kelly and lighting designer Thomas Kelly. (Loewenstein had worked with these two design professionals in nearby Pinehurst on the Tate Residence.) Loewenstein also retained the services of a landscape architect, John V. Townsend, as the building required careful consideration of garden and adjacent spaces to expand occupiable spaces beyond the walls of the home.

For his most highly complex dwelling, Loewenstein used a similar Modernist idiom as at the Carter and Bertling residences, but he took the design approaches and considerations to a whole new level. Because he designed the building for himself, he experienced few client restraints, other than balancing his more Modern world and the eclectic one appreciated by his wife. As with other commissions, Loewenstein listened well and brought into being a sophisticated and successful scheme. Made possible by this ability to experiment and because of the large size of the structure, many more of Loewenstein's design influences can be seen his own residence. In the building, Loewenstein more completely demonstrated the influence of Frank Lloyd Wright's connection to the land, Walter Gropius's Bauhaus ideals of formal exploration, and Ludwig Mies van der Rohe's penchant for clean, uncluttered living. Featured in the *New York Times Magazine* (June 1955), the house remained an archetype of his personal style and design approach.

Distinguishing his house from earlier commissions, Loewenstein more completely separated the spatial experiences between private and public. He opened the public spaces by including clerestory windows and large window walls that connected the various rooms to the outdoors. As a result, he incorporated a spine of light to stitch together the complex public spaces. Varying during the day and through the seasons, the light quality entering these openings and the ability to catch a glimpse of trees and the sky outside offered an experience of ever-changing senses of the interior connected to a world beyond. Further

This axonometric drawing includes a conceptualization of a roof plane (never built) to connect the main structure to the carport. Note the tree on the right side of the composition embedded within the structure. The signature sloping walls are apparent in this drawing along the left side of the scheme and in the clerestory windows that signify the center light spine running along the east-west breadth of the structure. (LAA)

underscoring this fluidity, Loewenstein incorporated a curved stone wall between dining room and living room that, like the front entrance wall of the Carter commission, simultaneously screened and embraced, drawing the infinite and the intimate into one world. Though visitors experienced this more open nature of the home in the public spaces, here they found no doubled living space (as at the Carters').

As in earlier commissions, Loewenstein included a similar palette of materials indoors and out, connecting the interior experience to the outdoors. He exposed structural elements, taking the cue from early experimentation at Carter and Bertling. Here the steel angled I-beams that support the living room ceiling show an architect between two worlds — one embracing the machine aesthetic of high Modernism but tempering that aesthetic with the careful fabrication of the beam, which has been split in two along a diagonal, one element reversed and welded back together to achieve the tapered shape.

Showing maturation from earlier commissions, Loewenstein designed a more extensive system of built-in cabinets in all areas of the house. In the public rooms, he inserted book shelves as a divider between the living room and guest room wall. Interestingly, he did not include built-in storage in the dining room, though he did include a "butler's pantry" adjacent to the kitchen for storing china and silver. In this service area, Loewenstein planned a kitchen, breakfast room, bar, butler's pantry, laundry area, and maid's room. Quite similar to the Carter Residence in both size and form, these service spaces provided ease of occupation and use for the family and servants. In the private areas of the house, Loewenstein incorporated built-in cabinets and closets. He also used these architectural components as space dividers and entryways to the bedrooms. In each case, the storage system and the bathrooms insulated bedrooms from the circulation spine, providing a greater degree of privacy to the residents.

The design team adopted strategies for softening the Modern appearance of the building by celebrating materials and finishes. Ann Tate actually encouraged Loewenstein to take advantage of Sarah Hunter Kelly's interiors knowledge, dropping him a note that said: "I think it would be ideal if Mrs. Kelly could work with Frances," referring to Loewenstein's wife.[21] From all accounts, Kelly worked with Mrs. Loewenstein closely as the matron of the household assembled a vision for the residence, which, after the Tate commission, represented Loewenstein's most far-reaching Modern work, complete with sloping full-glass exterior walls, an open plan, and a strong formal unfolding of the building in

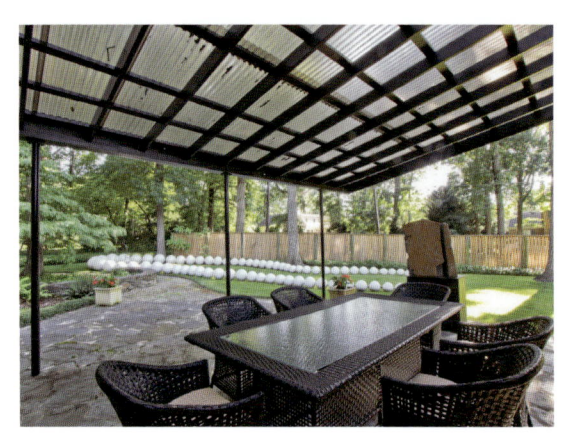

Outside "rooms" form, bounded by low stone walls, overhead roof planes, and plantings. These extensions of internal living space provide easy transitions for residents and guests, and link the interior and exterior experience into a seamless one. The trees in the wooded lot provide vertical contrasts to the horizontal sweep of the house (*top left*). As at the Bertling Residence, Loewenstein specified corrugated fiberglass for the covered exterior space adjacent to the living room (*bottom left*). Upon exiting the house, the circular carport closes the view and creates an additional experience of being indoors within an outdoor space (*below*). (*top left*: PLL; *bottom left*: CTB; *below*: PLL)

Moss takes over as a soft texture in the natural world in the outdoor "room" outside the living room. Shifting seasonally, the wooded site provides a buffer to adjoining properties. The terrace outside the living room and dining room, partly under roof, supplies sheltered spaces for outside living during temperate seasons. The corrugated fiberglass roof overhead allows light to stream into the patio and the living room beyond. (CTB)

Typical of many residences, Loewenstein situates the house on a large wooded lot, with the entrance hidden from the road. The driveway and walkways meandered in a curving line from the road to the carport to the main entrance. The organic and selective curves meshed well with the immediate surroundings of the wooded lot. At the front entrance, the stone from the exterior walkway continues into the foyer, slipping under the slanted glass wall to the left of the front door. Similar to his other residential designs, the foyer immediately opens to the public space of the welcoming living room. A steel sculpture, collected by the current residents of the home, provides the visual focus for the front entrance terrace. The stepping corbels of brick in the view show the edge of the bedroom wing and the presence of the hallmark canted walls on this archetypal residence. (CTB)

This 1974 photograph of front entry court demonstrates the visual impact of the architect's desire to maintain trees extant on the site within the composition of the home. The planting materials provide privacy to the large series of glass planes that sit at the edge of the entry cross hall. Visitors enter the structure through the front door, on the right. (Danny Fafard)

a carefully sited landscape. Balancing the Modern views of the husband-architect with the eclecticism favored by the wife must have been a significant challenge for Kelly. By borrowing on her design philosophy of "good taste," though, she achieved a relative harmony within the house's interiors, articulating a vision that accommodated antiques alongside contemporary seating and case pieces that accentuated and celebrated a Modern envelope.

From Kelly came the mediating influences of textures and colors in the brightly patterned textiles as both upholstery and, most significantly, curtain surfaces. When drawn, the open landscapes slipped from view, bringing a comfort and warmth to the open plan in the relief from the bold forms of the architectural enclosure. By closing the curtain panels, one experienced a whole new layer of richness relative to surface and pattern in an already complex environment. This kind of design strategy, however, brought a special character to the interior and grounded the human experience of space in varied and subtle ways. Key to the mix here was Kelly's husband, Thomas, who designed lighting fixtures and effects throughout the house, as had been the case with the Tate Residence. Placing washes of light across the patterned textiles more boldly accented their place as an active design element, most notably in the living room where a printed fabric, used for furniture upholstery as well as at the windows, featured an "image taken from a contemporary painting of Loches Cathedral in France," on "linen in dull green and charcoal, with touches of brick, on a pale blue ground."[22] Collaborating with Thomas Kelly, Loewenstein incorporated fluorescent fixtures on rheostats in light troughs for nighttime lighting, a detail he would later employ in nearly every residential commission over the next two decades.

Along with lighting techniques designed by her husband, Kelly's palette of materials and textures and the highly sophisticated enclosing envelope visualized by Loewenstein and carried out by more than a handful of firm employees, suggested a plurality of vision in the interior. At the center of all of those decisions stood Kelly with Frances Loewenstein; together they debated the merits of furnishing choices, artwork, and accessories throughout making the unusual house of the South "as appropriate as a white-columned mansion."[23] Kelly was most certainly part of that successful blending of past and present by bringing good taste to North Carolina in a wide-ranging and diverse approach to the furnishings and finishes on this house interior.[24] Above all, this house represented a social web of connections, in which both husband-architect and wife, as well as myriad design professionals, craftsmen, builders, and installers, easily juxtaposed styles across several genres, making spaces and furnishings easily livable and somehow more appealing than strictly Modern or traditional spaces in contemporaneous projects.

As with the Carter Residence and the Bertling Residence, Loewenstein separated public and private space through space planning and division. Based on these earlier experiments, he further compartmentalized the sense of space in the private sectors of the house through more extensive use of built-in closets and storage units. Though connected to previous commissions, Loewenstein clarified organization in the house through the use of a long hallway to organize the private spaces along one wing. The bedrooms, in a wing to the left of the main entrance, maintain social distance from rooms for entertaining — the living room, dining room, and front hall. Thus, the floor plan for the Loewenstein residence reflects the consolidation of the architect's design ideas while also illustrating public-private dichotomies and utilizing built-ins to reinforce design strategies. (LAA)

The angles and placement of the large and clerestory windows throughout the house resulted from sun studies to mitigate the hot summer sun and take advantage of winter's warm rays as the sunlight shifts through the seasons. These studies affected the design of the home in myriad ways, resulting in an almost forced perspective of inside being drawn out through the resultant angled walls and reducing the glare within the interior. With its expansive glass walls that brought the exterior landscape into the space, Loewenstein situated the public rooms to take full advantage of the landscape, with the fireplace as a focal point in the house (a page taken from Wright) situated along a large window but not obscuring the view (*left*). Echoing his earlier commissions, Loewenstein specified a similar materials palette for his own home: honey-colored wood for ceilings and walls in the public spaces, plaster walls in private and service spaces; a curving Carolina fieldstone wall between the living and dining rooms (*right*); and cork, stone, carpet, and vinyl tile floors. Sarah Hunter Kelly supplemented the warm color palette from the architectural envelope with furnishings and finishes that further emphasized a human quality to them throughout. (*left*, David Wilson / *UNCG Magazine*; *right*, CTB)

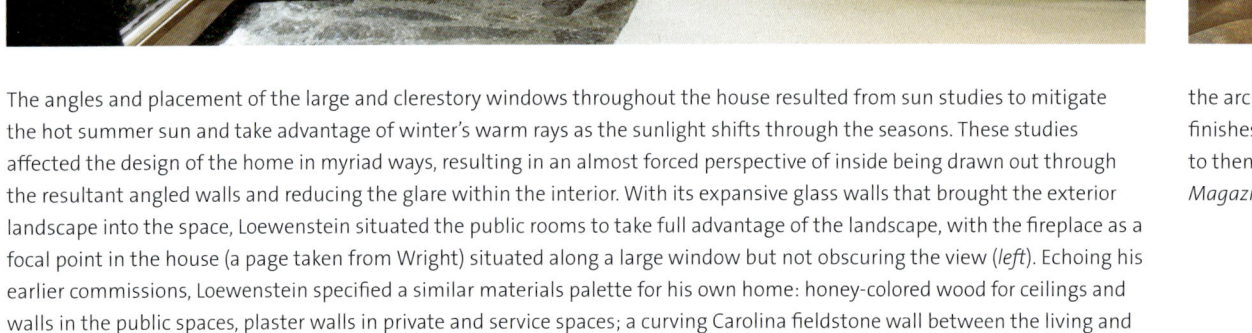

From the pool area, the orderly composition marked by varying segments of the building — the bedroom wing to the left, the den in the center, the entrance court, and the kitchen wing to the right — signals the distinct horizontal orientation of the composition. With the hydrangeas in this late spring view and other planting materials, the building settles into its wooded lot. Ralph, the beloved dog of the current owners adds an element of playfulness and a canine scale to the scene (*left*). The slanted exterior walls of the house appear prominent upon approach to the house as those who approach continue to enjoy the groundedness of the design in its verdant landscape in the dappled shade (*above*). The layers of the house unfold above with the presence of the clerestory windows of the living room. At night, the light washes from these windows, apparent upon approach, lend a playful quality to the composition. (CTB)

The Loewenstein Residence shows multiple design influences interweaving with the dispositions of the architect's collaborators, Sarah Hunter Kelly and Thomas Smith Kelly. In the living room, Sarah Hunter Kelly helped develop multiple seating areas, furnished with streamlined upholstered pieces along with other specified furnishings. The paper and metal lantern, one of two in the space, lends interest to the sweeping diagonal ceiling structurally supported by the hand-made flanged beams. The fan-powered ventilation system of the fireplace, to the right, permits the location of the working firebox in a glass wall, thus freeing the view from any structural restriction. Under Loewenstein's direction, his engineer designed the vent for the fireplace to burrow underground and rise up again several yards from the house, leaving the view open on this important façade of the living room wall. (CTB)

Sarah Hunter Kelly specified the dining room furnishings, attributed to French furniture designer Jacques Adnet. The Colonial light fixture converses with the modern table and accompanying sideboard, all furnishings specified or accounted for by Kelly. Light sweeps in from the clerestory windows on the right, highlighting the fieldstone wall and providing ambience to the table at which meals are enjoyed. (CTB)

The Loewenstein Residence was featured in the 19 June 1955 *New York Times Magazine*. Writer Betty Pepis notes "In a part of the country renowned for its traditional homes, the contemporary house shown here is particularly notable. Although it is unusual for the South, careful planning has made it seem just as appropriate as a white-columned mansion." Note the continuity of the furnishings in these images compared to the present-day images in this catalog. (*New York Times Magazine*)

Adjacent to the kitchen, a bar greets visitors as part of the entry sequence at the Loewenstein Residence. A signature amenity of mid-century entertaining, guests to the home paused for a libation before proceeding to the living room and its stunning landscape views. (CTB)

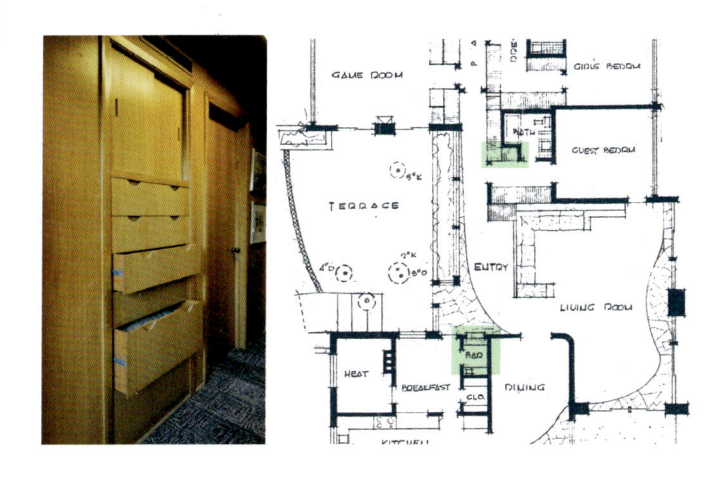

Built-in storage, in the hallway leading to the guest bedroom, demonstrates the economy of internal planning so characteristic of Loewenstein dwellings. In both floor plan and experience, this use of storage works like an aural and visual barrier for these private rooms. (*left*, CTB; *right*, LAA)

49

JULIET + OSCAR BURNETT RESIDENCE : GREENSBORO (1954)

In the hybrid house, existing somewhere between the traditional dwelling and the Modern residence, Loewenstein and his firm attempted balance between two design views.[25] In these dwellings, Loewenstein linked materials, light, and color; interior furnishings; building systems; exterior site relationships and landscape features; and design philosophies into seamless stories, stories that relied on both traditional and Modern elements within the same building. Because of their variety and the porous nature of the stylistic boundaries they encapsulated, these hybrid houses help us to understand multiple Modernisms as regional and local variations on international themes, rather than a single Modernism without context, site condition, or client. Like the pure Modernist dwellings, Loewenstein's hybrid houses revealed the harmonious interaction of design elements with one another.

Located on a cul-de-sac populated by three ranch houses and two other Loewenstein houses with more traditional leanings, the Burnett Residence maintains a vestigial gable facing the street. The front door, to the right of the gable, sits beneath a line of clerestory windows and pierced roof openings — a bit more obscured and less obvious an entrance, taking a cue from Loewenstein's Modern dwellings. Moreover, the wide overhanging eaves (approximately 30") that surround the house and contribute to the horizontal emphasis of the scheme clearly borrow from Modernist-style dwellings he designed elsewhere in the neighborhood. As was the case with his Modern dwellings, Loewenstein connected the interior and exterior by creating patios, porches, walks and drives easily accessible from different parts of the house. Large south-facing, sliding and fixed-glass windows increase the perceived spaciousness in the home, maximizing views to the outside. Except for a few fixed-pane windows, standard-issue awning windows rather than custom-built ones allowed air to flow through the house while keeping the elements out.

In this 5,000 square foot home, Loewenstein arranged the public core of shared spaces at the center with the bedrooms and quiet spaces at the periphery, all well appointed with storage and daily necessities to suit various hobbies and frequent entertaining. In hybrid houses like the Burnett Residence, Loewenstein specified more practical than lavish finishes and materials for the interior, celebrating the patterns of natural materials, for example, when the active pattern of the wood grain meets the equally lively travertine surround of the living room fireplace. Uniform interior trim sets a minimal aesthetic throughout the house.

hybrid

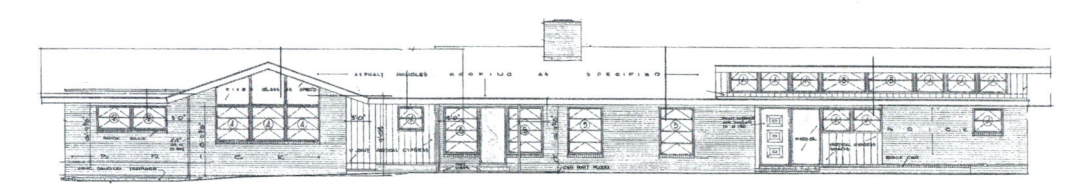

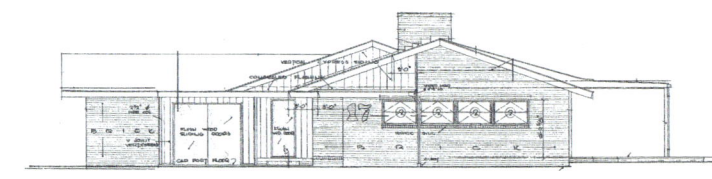

The front and right side elevations show how Loewenstein negotiated between traditional and Modern vocabulary. Clerestory windows and a horizontal orientation contrast the gable end of the recreation room on the front façade. The sides of the house conform to more typical suburban models rather than the flat roof planes of his more Modern commissions. (LAA)

The street view of the Burnett Residence (*top*) shows the front-facing gable (a vestige of the traditional buildings in the area). The general horizontal orientation of the building in the landscape and the landscape features underscore a more Modern approach to design. The west façade of the dwelling (*bottom*), what Loewenstein labeled as the clerestory wing, demonstrates a decidedly more Modern aesthetic. (PLL)

Consistent with plan types for hybrid houses, the floor plan (1952), slightly amended for construction (1954), tends toward centralization and permeability, reinforced by strategic service spaces and built-ins and grounded by a central chimney, a signpost for the public, shared spaces within the house. Visitors enter the structure through a small hall on the right side of the plan from which they proceed to the large living room. A long hallway, reminiscent of other Loewenstein houses, leads to the children's wing and recreation room. Located to the right of the entrance, the master bedroom remains separate from the children's wing, but the private spaces join the public at the two ends of the plan. (LAA)

51

The front entrance (*above left*) is located beneath a line of clerestory windows and a broad overhanging eave pierced with openings, classic Loewenstein repertoire for Modernism on the North Carolina landscape. The broad width of the overhang throughout the house (*above right*) casts strong horizontal shadows, further emphasizing ties to the landscape and standing in strong contrast to the vertically oriented traditional buildings of the suburbs. (PLL)

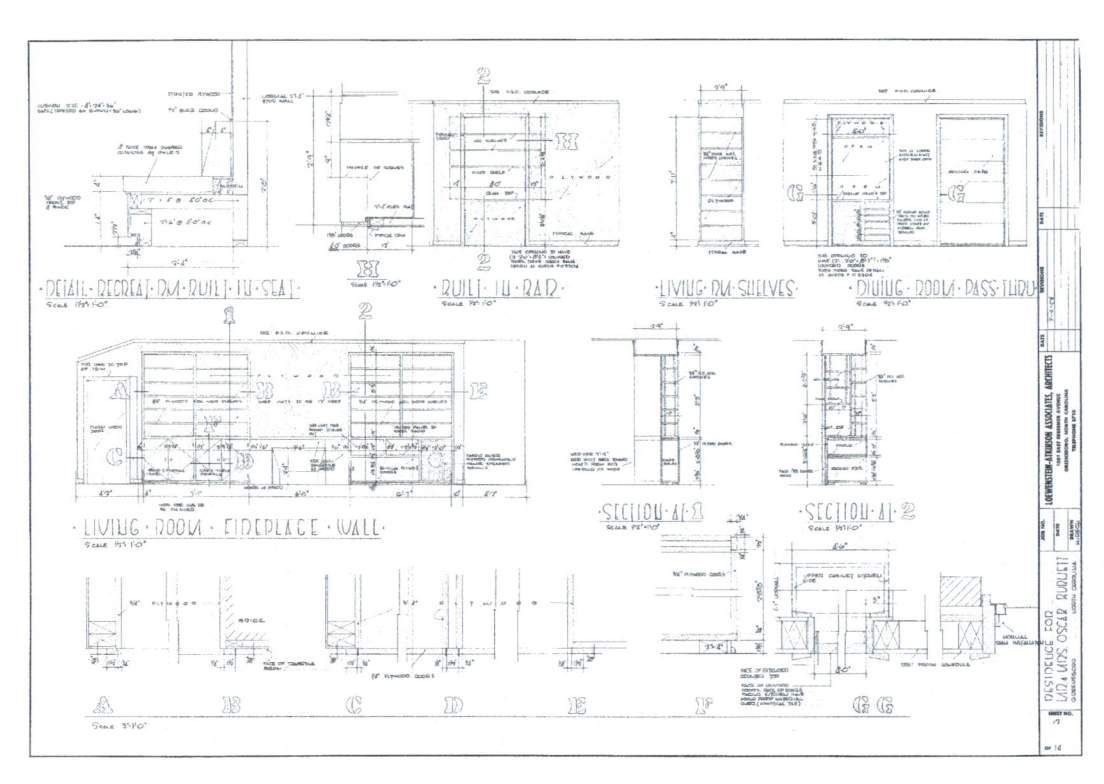

The long narrow hallway in the bedroom wing (*left*) and the built-in storage cabinets, drawers, and convenience surfaces in one of the bedrooms (*far left*) are both reminiscent of Loewenstein's Modern structures. For this home, he used the long corridor as an organizational principle (a nod to his Modern homes), but here the lack of a maid's quarter sets up a new dichotomy. Loewenstein connected the children's wing and rec room to this hall leading to public core while he set the master bedroom apart from it, on the opposite end of the house from the public core by the sitting room, located just beyond the entry hall. (PLL)

In the drawing set (*above*), three of the twelve sheets include specifications for the built-in cabinetry throughout the house. Commensurate with his interest in built-in storage as space divider and space saver, Loewenstein considered practical and functional storage closets in nearly every room of the Burnett Residence: the halls, bedrooms, rec room, carport with its garden storage, heater room with log storage, whole built-in storage walls in the living room, and a broom closet off of the main entry next to the kitchen. (LAA)

notes

1. Richard L. Bushman, *The Refinement of America: Persons, Houses, Cities* (New York, 1993).

2. During the 1950s, the number of cars in the U.S. nearly doubled from 39 million to 74 million and by 1960, 80% of American families owned at least one car and 15% owned two or more. J. Ronald Oakley, *God's Country : America in The Fifties* (New York, 1986), p. 239.

3. John Stilgoe, *Borderland: Origins of the American Suburb*, 1820-1939 (New Haven, CT, 1988).

4. John Archer, *Architecture and Suburbia: From English Villa to American Dream House, 1690-2000* (Minneapolis, MN, 2005).

5. Elizabeth O'Leary offers a compelling argument for the intertwined nature of domestics and householders in the nineteenth-century residence. The shared space and functionality of the household continued in the twentieth century as a means to stitch together people of different economic, racial, and social groups. O'Leary, *At Beck and Call: The Representation of Domestic Servants in Nineteenth-Century American Painting* (Washington, DC, 1996).

6. Karal Ann Marling, *As Seen on TV: The Visual Culture of Everyday Life in the 1950s* (Cambridge, MA, 1996).

7. Sandy Isenstadt, *The Modern American House: Spaciousness and Middle-Class Identity* (Cambridge, UK, 2006).

8. George, Teyssot, ed., *The American Lawn* (New York, 1999).

9. Isenstadt, *The Modern American House*.

10. Anne Massey, *Interior Design since 1900*, 3rd ed. (London, 2010).

11. Judith Attfield, *Wild Things: The Material Culture of Everyday Life* (London, 2000).

12. Marling, *As Seen on TV*.

13. Modern dwellings only appeared in the popular press as an exception rather than a rule. In a visual survey of *Architectural Record* (trade journal) and *House and Garden Magazine* (popular press) from the 1950s, the disparity between traditional and Modern dwellings increased in distance and breadth throughout the decade. Jennifer René Tate and Madeline Farlow conducted research on these periodicals in 2006 and 2011, respectively, under the auspices of the UNCG Office of Undergraduate Research Grants program.

14. Through his books on American taste and manners, both satirical and popular, Lynes criticized American conservative preferences in art and architecture along with a general ridicule of pretentious people. See *The Tastemakers* (New York, 1983), which was first published serially in *Harper's* in the 1950s.

15. Preliminary sketches of a Modern house in the Loewenstein-Atkinson archives (private collection, Greensboro, NC, hereafter LAA) indicate that the 1947 James E. Hart Residence on Westridge Road predates the Carter Residence as Loewenstein's first Modernist building. Hart served as a partner in the engineering firm that shared the building where Loewenstein kept his offices. Poor street and parcel numbers on Westridge, at that time outside the Greensboro city limits, prevent determining the exact location of the home, which likely no longer stands. Three residences by Loewenstein or Loewenstein-Atkinson took shape on the same street between 1957 and 1965. Only one survives in a radically altered form, thus preventing any further documentation from being gathered about the Modern qualities of the structures other than the limited resources in the firm archives for these commissions.

16. "Room for Living," *Greensboro Record*, January 12, 1952. Firm memo, Loewenstein to Douglass, June 1952, LAA. A later note indicates that Molitor visited Greensboro on 16-17 November of that year and completed the photographs.

17. "Residence for Mr. and Mrs. Wilbur L. Carter, Jr., Greensboro, N. C.," *Architectural Record* 112 (November 1952): 190-92. "Residence for Mr. and Mrs. W. L. Carter, Jr., Greensboro," *Southern Architect* 1 (March 1955): 21.

18. Loewenstein to Florence A. Van Wyck, 23 September 1952, LAA.

19. Oral history interview with Wilbur Carter Jr., Greensboro, NC, 10 September 2007. Cynthia de Miranda reports in additional email correspondence with Lee Carter (November 2007) that *AR* erroneously published the story. "Wilbur and Martha Carter Residence," National Register Nomination, 2010.

20. Loewenstein to Florence A. Van Wyck, 23 September 1952, LAA.

21. Ann Tate to Loewenstein, 9 February 1952, LAA.

22. Betty Pepis, "Modern House Down South," *New York Times* 19 June 1955.

23. Ibid.

24. Jane Loewenstein Levy interview conducted by the author, 27 April 2007.

25. Working as an undergraduate research assistant in 2008–2009, Ashley Warriner Andrews interpreted a handful of houses in one section of Irving Park. I base the detailed analysis of the Burnett Residence on the foundations she laid in her yearlong project and extend my thanks for her smart reading of the houses based on an approach centered in material culture and visual analysis.

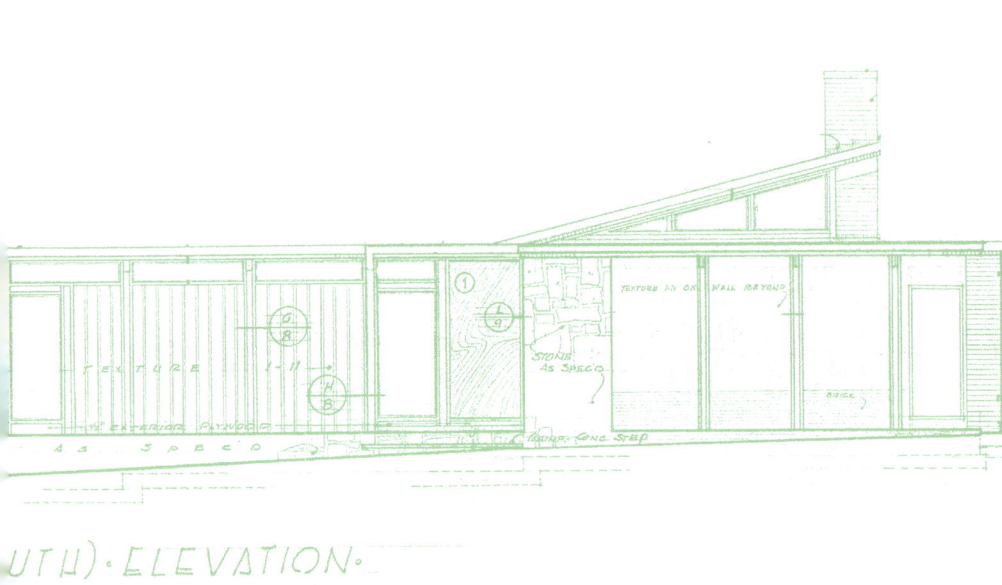

beyond plantation nostalgia

though North Carolina has a rich history in traditional folk art, mixing Native American and European art in the Western mountains, in the Piedmont region, and in the maritime commerc[ial] areas down East, citizens of the Tar Heel state never deeply embraced Modernism. And yet, traditions in pottery, quilting, woodworking, and textiles handed down through families represented similar practices to Bauhaus philosophies in the connection between head and han[d], design and craft, and truth in materials, especially in the craft schools of Western Carolina. But where these craft traditions manifested themselves through work of the last two centuries, Modernism's contemporary threads have become embedded only as an accent to the more common architectural expression of traditional dwellings throughout the state.

MODERNISM IN NORTH CAROLINA

Three significant concentrations of Modernist design in North Carolina contribute to an understanding of Modernism in the South: the buildings designed by faculty and associates of t[he] North Carolina State University School of Design in Raleigh; the buildings designed by the Web[b] Brothers in Chapel Hill; and the more general influence of the faculty at the Black Mountain College near Asheville. Because these pockets of Modernism existed in relative isolation from ea[ch] other, Loewenstein's work represents an understudied link within North Carolina Modernism a[nd] can help readers see Modernism as a reality in the South.

By helping make Modernism "at home" in the Piedmont, Loewenstein worked to raise the regional architectural tradition beyond plantation nostalgia. His work provides a rare deviance from the traditionally styled buildings of North Carolina communities. Even within his own firm, the Modern residential work represents only a small fraction of Loewenstein's own designs[,] and the firm's accomplishments in Greensboro and beyond, which responded to a traditionally minded clientele. Of the 1,600 commissions between 1952 and 1970, the firm drew plans for approximately 400 residential buildings. Of those, only 50 stood as examples of mid-century Modernism, indicating that only a few exceptional clients accepted Modernist residential desig[n]. Loewenstein's unique houses were even more cutting-edge within a community that valued the tried and true. He may have represented a dissenting voice among his fellow architects in the Piedmont and among the small network of practitioners in North Carolina, yet by adding to th[e] regional building vocabulary and architectural language, Loewenstein's Modern aesthetics revea[l a] shifting landscape in the South.

In Raleigh in 1948, North Carolina State University hired Henry L. Kamphoefner, an architecture professor from the University of Oklahoma, to lead a new school of architecture an[d] design. Kamphoefner hired a number of faculty members who would be influential in defining North Carolina Modernism: George Matsumoto, Matthew Nowicki, James Fitzgibbon, Duncan Stuart, Eduardo Catalano, Milton Small, Edward Waugh, and John Latimer.[1] Through their effor[ts] to disseminate Modernism's message to students and their building designs in Raleigh, Chapel Hill, and beyond, these faculty members advanced Modernism's cause in traditional North Carolina east of Greensboro.

At the same time, changes were afoot at the University of North Carolina (UNC) in Chapel Hill. James Murray (Jim) Webb helped found UNC's city and regional planning program beginning in 1947. Webb had studied at MIT and worked for San Francisco architect William Wurster. In 1957, Jim's brother John, who also had worked for Wurster, joined him at UNC. The two brought Wurster's Bay Area regional Modernist vernacular to Chapel Hill in a dozen residences primarily for UNC faculty in the Laurel Hill, Westwood, Greenwood neighborhoods, as well as in new subdivisions in Whitehead Circle, Glendale, Coker Hills, and Lake Forest Estates.[2]

A decade or two before, in the 1930s and 1940s, the establishment of a new experimental college near Asheville had brought international artists to North Carolina, many of whom were refugees from war-torn Europe. Black Mountain College (1933–1957) demonstrated the promise of Modernism as a beacon of pioneering ideas and explorations led by German-born artist Josef Albers. Albers brought many of the teaching ideals from the Bauhaus and helped develop a fusion of Modernism and progressive explorations in a deeply intellectual and creative community. Among the many artists to teach and study there were Walter Gropius, Willem de Kooning, Barbara Morgan, R. Buckminster Fuller, Cy Twombly, and Robert Rauschenberg. Black Mountain College teachers introduced their students to areas like action painting, existential art, pop art, décollage and assemblage, beat art, pop art, and kinetic art.[3]

In Greensboro, as we have seen, Loewenstein emerged as the main voice for Modernism, first as a sole practitioner and then with the various employees of the Loewenstein-Atkinson firm who espoused Modernist design approaches. Though Loewenstein represented the only Modern voice in residential work, he was not the only source for the design of Modern commercial buildings in the community. Prior to Loewenstein's arrival, Greensboro had seen Modernism in the forms of the American Container Corporation Warehouse (1943–1944) on East Market Street, attributed to Walter Gropius, and the Ellis Stone Department Store (1949) downtown, designed by the New York firm Vorhees, Walker, Foley, and Smith. In the 1960s, Loewenstein watched as both of A. G. Odell's designs took shape for the Wachovia Bank Building (1966) downtown and the Burlington Industries Corporate Headquarters (1971) at Friendly Center, with its distinct external structure.[4] Eduardo Catalano received the commission for the City-County Building complex (1968–1972), and Edward Durrell Stone completed plans for the High Point City Hall (1975), both commissions built after Loewenstein's death. Late in his life, Loewenstein also competed for commissions with practicing architects in Greensboro, including two firms, McMinn, Norfleet, and Wicker and J. Hyatt Hammond, the latter continuing to produce Modern commercial work after Loewenstein died.[5]

In Modern residential work, Loewenstein competed with some contractors who offered housing to property owners without hiring an architect. For example, many of the Modernist-inspired residences in Starmount Forest and Hamilton Lakes neighborhoods have been attributed to the builder J. Hiatt. His own residence on Friendly Avenue speaks to some of the tenets of Modernism, including horizontality, innovative use of materials, lack of historic ornament, and sensitive siting.[6] Superior Construction Company, with Eugene Gulledge as its head, built several residential and commercial commissions for Loewenstein-Atkinson. As a collaborator, Gulledge brought in subcontractors and laborers and formed a satellite network to realize many of the firm's innovative residential and commercial designs.[7]

SEEKING PARTNERS IN MODERNISM

During his early years of solo practice in the Piedmont, Loewenstein attempted partnerships with two New York firms, Peter Copeland (Albany) and Telchin and Campanella Architects (New York City) and tried to forge collaborations with several North Carolina State University School of Design faculty members. Of course, the most successful collaboration was with Robert A. Atkinson Jr., who had worked for Loewenstein as a draftsman from 1947 and 1952, and joined in a partnership in 1953. Their successful business employed 25 to 35 employees from the mid-1950s until 1970. Though most of the commissions were in Greensboro and Guilford County, the firm experimented with a series of satellite offices in nearby Burlington, Reidsville, and Sanford, North Carolina, as well as Martinsville and Danville, Virginia. Further afield, they tried offices in Wilmington and Raleigh, the latter associated with Edward Waugh, then a faculty member at the North Carolina School of Design. These satellite offices drew significant expense from the central business in Greensboro and by the mid-1950s all had closed, except Burlington, which remained open through the mid-1960s under the careful direction of architect Vernon E. Lewis.[8]

The several dozen interns and employees who worked

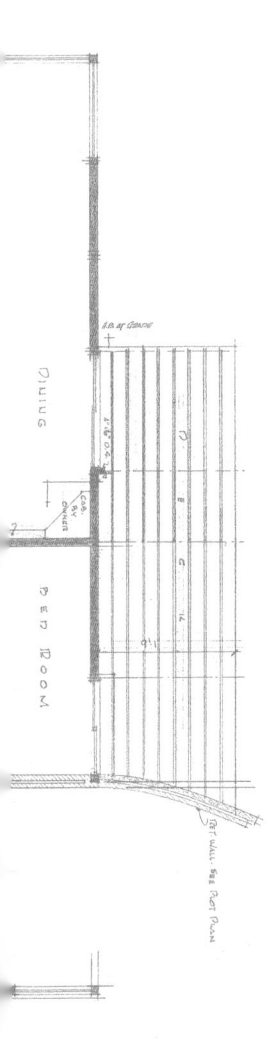

with Loewenstein in Greensboro amplified his own vision of Modernism.⁹ Employee documents and job lists show a variety of tasks and jobs assigned in several key areas: administration, structural and engineering tasks, job management, specifications, and interior design. In all of these documents, Loewenstein remained the key contact for clients, Atkinson assumed much of the responsibility for day-to-day management of the office, a cadre of engineers and draftsmen carried out the everyday tasks of the design firm, and critical clerical staff provided support for the firm, the latter group led capably for many years by Virginia Bright.

Several Loewenstein employees went on to establish their own firms, placing onto the landscape later examples of residential Modernism in the community, most notably the young African-American architects W. Edward Jenkins and Clinton Gravely. Willie Edward Jenkins (1923–1988) earned his B.S. in Architectural Engineering from North Carolina A&T State University in 1949. He was hired at Loewenstein-Atkinson after graduation on the recommendation of a black employee, William Gupple, who recommended Jenkins for the job since he was not able to find one elsewhere.¹⁰ Within five years Jenkins had worked from an entry position as draftsman to associate architect. Upon receiving his architectural registration (with a reference letter from Loewenstein to the AIA board), Jenkins established his own firm in 1962.¹¹ Clinton Gravely (1935–) was born into a Reidsville contractor family and attended college at Howard University, where he earned a bachelors degree in Architecture in 1959.¹² With no firms in Reidsville willing to hire Gravely, Loewenstein stepped in, offering him a position at his firm in 1962. After a few years experience, Gravely established his own firm in Greensboro, Clinton E. Gravely and Associates, in 1967. At Loewenstein-Atkinson, Gravely worked, among other commissions, on the **Leah and A. J. Tannenbaum Residence** (1963), designing many of the interiors and details, and the **Hargett Funeral Home** (1965).¹³

While at Loewenstein-Atkinson, Jenkins designed the gymnasium for **Dudley High School** (1959), then a school for African-American students. The innovation of a steel-frame groin vault earned Jenkins and the firm accolades from the National Association of School Architects and the American Institute of Steel Construction. Jenkins was also lead architect on the **St. James Presbyterian Church** (1959), another of the firm's projects centered in the black community. In a moonlight commission outside the firm, Jenkins designed the J. Kenneth Lee Residence (1959) for a well-known civil rights attorney, incorporating many of the Modernist features in other Loewestein-Atkinson commissions: horizontal emphasis, clerestory windows, and vertical paneling. These projects exemplify Loewenstein's efforts to promote talent from within the firm, regardless of race. Often this practice led to Loewenstein establishing young architects in firms of their own, as was the case with Jenkins and Gravely.¹⁴

Ellen Kjosnes Cash worked at the firm the summers of 1953 and 1954 and was "smitten [with Loewenstein] because he believed in women. There was not a man at that time who would have admitted to that."¹⁵ Clearly Loewenstein not only worked beyond borders of race but also advanced the firm's stance on gender equity in design. One of Loewenstein's students when he taught at Woman's College, designer Anne Bowers (One Design Center, Greensboro) remains active in historic preservation because of Loewenstein's teaching. Countless others settled in North Carolina and beyond, including Anne Greene, who founded a successful practice in Washington, D.C. In reflecting on her mentor, Greene stated: "Little did I know that once I met Ed Loewenstein that my world would expand beyond my wildest dreams. . . . Hopefully I have been a link in continuing his legacy."¹⁶

Thomas P. Heritage served as structural engineer in the firm before beginning his own practice in the 1950s. The firm offered design services in engineering as well as in architecture, and increasingly the engineering work equalled and then surpassed the architecture commissions. In partnership with Loewenstein in the years before his death, Tom Wilson collaborated on a number of key engineering projects and he continues the firm's practice as Wilson + Lysiak today. Frank Harmon, interning in 1963–1964, drafted plans and crafted light fixtures for the **Leah and A. J. Tannenbaum Residence**. He later founded his own successful firm and continues practice today in Raleigh as a well-known architect in the state.

Both inside and outside the firm, an important and influential partnership developed between Loewenstein and artist Gregory Ivy, a career-long friend. As Chairman of Woman's College's Department of Art, Ivy invited Loewenstein to teach in 1958, and the two embarked on an unprecedented plan to lead young women out of the insular design studio and into the community as they designed and built the Commencement Houses. Through these projects Loewenstein and Ivy planted the seed of cooperation and collaboration in young women, empowering them to do more than they ever imagined. Gregory Ivy served as the Interior Coordinator for the third house, though from a position within the Loewenstein-Atkinson firm, as he had departed from Woman's College in 1961. Not only did Ivy assist with the

Commencement Houses, he also provided design services and had manufactured significant furniture designs for the **Evelyn and John Hyman Residence** (1959) under the employ of the firm. At the **Greensboro Public Library** (1964) Ivy designed and had fabricated large-scale concrete relief panels for the Greene Street and Friendly Avenue facades of the building, as well as supervising the selection of a number of the interior appointments, mostly in the public spaces of the structure.

Another local ally was Otto Zenke of Otto Zenke Inc. (Interior Decorators, Antiques, Reproductions). Among other commissions, Loewenstein and Zenke together designed the **Edythe and Herman L. Davidson Residence** (ca. 1956) in the Starmount Forest neighborhood, where Zenke's French Provincial Revival style in both living and dining rooms at the front of the house masked a mid-century Modern kitchen, family room, and bedroom wing opening to the rear.

On several important commissions (see chapter 2), Loewenstein partnered with Sarah Hunter Kelly, a prominent designer in New York City, and her husband-lighting designer, Thomas Kelly. The Kellys worked in Loewenstein's own house, the **Katherine and Sidney J. Stern, Jr. Residence** (1955–1956), and the **Leah and A. J. Tannenbaum Residence** (1963) in Greensboro, as well as on the **Ann and Lloyd P. Tate Residence** (1952) in Pinehurst. Sarah Kelly provided design services and specified traditional furniture pieces to soften the dwellings and to seamlessly integrate a comfortable family life within Loewenstein's mid-century Modern designs. Her husband's lighting schemes contributed greatly to the perception of a more softened Modernism in the dwellings. The resultant interiors — Edward Loewenstein's containers, Sarah Hunter Kelly's collections, and Thomas Kelly's lighting schemes — balanced design elements, resulting in a rich textural and visual experience, particularly within the public zones of the dwellings. Their livability in their design eclecticism appealed at mid-century and continue to do so today.[17]

In seeking collaborators for Modernism, Loewenstein's various partners and employees helped demonstrate how Modernism could dwell in the South. Certainly in Greensboro and in the various satellite offices, Loewenstein spread the ideas of Modernism in the state, but he was not the only architect to do so. His story from the Triad echoes similar efforts to bring Modernism to the South, whether from other regions (as Loewenstein himself came to North Carolina) or whether from training at a school of architecture that espoused Modernist philosophies. Through Loewenstein's service on the board of the North Carolina American Institute of Architects in the 1950s and his later service to the Architectural Foundation of North Carolina (to support the North Carolina State University School of Design), in his position as editor for *Southern Architect* (the publication of NCAIA), and through his occasional collaborative partnerships, Loewenstein linked to a network of like-minded Modern designers.

Often well hidden from the street on well-landscaped or tree-filled lots, organized around automobile culture, demonstrating close ties to the land through splendid siting, relying on natural light entering through large fenestration patterns, employing a strong horizontal emphasis in all aspects of the design, and making use of innovative new materials and regional ones, this loose network of Modern thinkers enlivened the landscape of the mid-century suburbs in Greensboro and throughout North Carolina. In Loewenstein's case, his vantage as a resident of Chicago and schooling in the North both contributed to his ability to see the community to which he moved with fresh eyes. In establishing a different aesthetic for houses in the postwar era, Loewenstein and his collaborators helped some forward-thinking clients to move beyond plantation nostalgia to a new paradigm for living.

VOICES IN THE SOUTHERN LANDSCAPE

For some in the South, Modern design seemed anathema to a world linked by tradition to its past, especially back to the Civil War and its aftermath. But like other sections of the county, the South received Modernism in pockets, with no wholesale adoption in any given community or neighborhood. In Greensboro, Modernism entered the landscape via newcomers to the South. The Cone family in particular, at the top of the social order, did not wholly embrace forward-thinking design but perhaps because of the modern manufacturing sense they forged in the community, they saw the need for houses that spoke the same language as their businesses: a more progressive vision for the future. They recognized that the tradition-loving South might not admire such a dramatic break from the past. In their houses, designers provided buildings that did cultural work both to ground with the past in material ways while still expressing openness and innovation in form and function. In casting aside the plantation traditions of the region, those involved with the textiles industry of the twentieth-century selected alternative aesthetic views.

Modernism in design, synonymous with change in social structures and understandings of the Greensboro community, comes at the time of the civil rights story, and Loewenstein stands squarely in the story as advocate and champion for disenfranchised members of the community. Though a movement not exclusive to the South, the communities and lunch counters of the region stood as the primary contested landscape in this national battle for equality. In Greensboro, individuals like Loewenstein worked at a local level to change the South's ways. Though he experienced some resistance from white employees of the firm who threatened to quit when he united the drafting facilities under a single roof for both whites and blacks, Loewenstein steadily advanced the place for African-Americans (and women) in the design fields. The houses he designed — and those designed by his collaborators — symbolized a spirit open to change and acceptance and, for this reason, they stood in contrast to their uptight and upright Classical- and Colonial-revival neighbors, houses that symbolized a connection to an idyllic past far from the realities of the inequalities for which they stood. Next to the columned mansions of the South, by the middle of the twentieth century, Modern dwellings like those designed by Loewenstein symbolized a new way of thinking about dwelling.

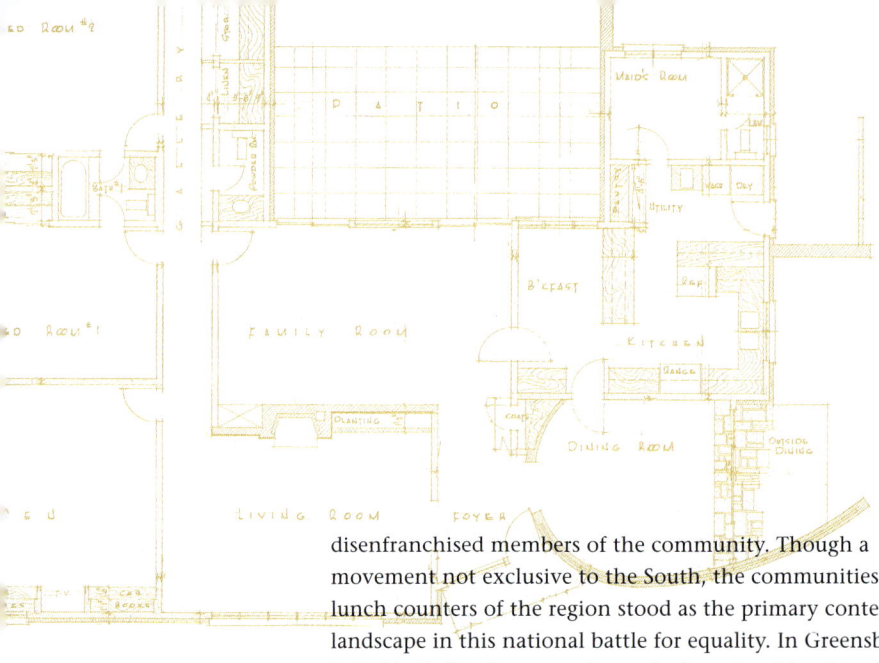

As in other sections of the nation, innovation met tradition in the residential South in suburban neighborhoods — and in houses by Loewenstein of the late 1950s. Given the boom in the economy and the corresponding number of housing starts after the close of World War II, residents of the South built new houses, primarily in traditional forms, just as their neighbors did to the North, by realizing their desire for traditional elements and details. Whether kit-built homes, in do-it-yourself mode, or contractor-built, residents selected styles across a wide range, mediating tradition with sometimes Modern details, ideas, materials, and planning strategies. More rarely, homeowners selected Modern sensibilities to shape a building to house their families. Some chose the popular Ranch style, some a more wholly Modern expression of architectural style, and some blended the two. Mediating somewhere between conformance to their neighbors and a desire for something different, neighborhood residents in Greensboro joined thousands of like-minded citizens across the region (and nation) in an exploration of an appropriate expression for twentieth-century living. The far fewer Modern schemes seem all the more unique popping up among their more traditional neighbors. Yet even those few Modern and Modern-leaning structures helped promote design solutions, and self-identifications, that reached beyond plantation nostalgia.

In the southern landscape, a place where the non-native plant, kudzu, flourishes — much to the concern of farmers — the notion of establishing new traditions in the New South becomes a reality. As outsiders (from the North and West) challenged the old guard, traditions were loosened and new voices were let in. From an architectural perspective, these pockets of Modernism — just as in other areas of the country — represented not a sweeping movement, but rather one that took root in selective ways. And we can begin to see some universality in the isolated and introspective pockets of Modernism. In Loewenstein's work, he explores his particular, localized expression of Modernism in a handful of additional houses built in the late 1950s.

KATHERINE + SIDNEY J. STERN, JR. RESIDENCE : GREENSBORO (1955)

The exterior of the Stern Residence floats on the landscape, blending into the natural environment through the use of cypress siding and warm red brick. The tri-level, Flemish-bond brick home incorporates a two-story front hall space accessed by large copper front doors. The sculptural staircase in the front hall connects all levels of the house and incorporates metal, open-tread risers cantilevered from a central structural element. Under a butterfly roof, the two-story portion of the composition features a series of bedrooms with corner windows to maximize the sense of sweeping light from the taller exterior walls to the shorter interior walls. Within the 5,000-square-foot structure, walls melt away replaced by large windows and sliding glass doors. On the back wall of the house, a gravel planting area blurs the architectural envelope, bringing the outside in, reinforced by gently curving changes in floor material, Carolina field stone slipping underneath sliding glass doors. Sarah Hunter Kelly's stylish furnishings enliven and animate the interior, providing color and texture that happily dialogue with Loewenstein's shell.

On the street façade, a stair hall sits behind copper-clad front doors encased within a two-story wood wall into which Loewenstein inserted large sheets of glass, thus revealing the "floating" staircase, a dramatic moment, highlighted by light and viewable from the street. The remainder of the front of the house remains closed behind brick and stained pecky cypress siding, further accentuating the drama of the staircase. A brick path and ample landscaping supplement the design for the front of the house, allowing it to nestle into the land and the wooded lot. The variety of texture and finish, the natural color palette, and the simplicity of forms bring the building subtly and softly onto the landscape. (CTB)

The rear façade of the Stern Residence shows the sweep of the composition across the well-manicured lawn, taking in the ample patio and water feature to the east side of the structure. The two-story anchor of the bedroom wing sits sturdily on the landscape. Sizable glass window walls opening from both the living room and the play room. Several large trees bring shade to the open patio and help to shape the outdoor experience near the house. A fishpond surrounded by naturalized plantings provides the focal point for this outdoor room. Patio tables with umbrellas further shade the space and bring color and texture variation to the east side of the building. (CTB)

59

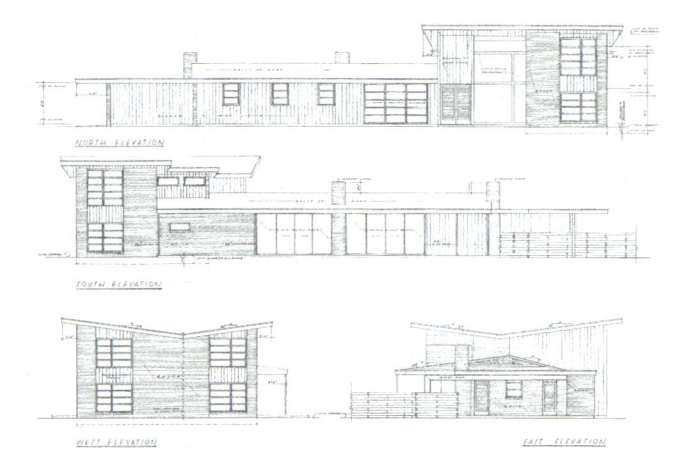

In contrast to many of Loewenstein's one-story plans, the two-story mass at the south end of the Stern Residence balances a lengthy, single story stretching to the north. These stacking, layered forms suggest a variety in experimentation with materials, light, and textures throughout the design. Where a butterfly roof tops the composition, its slightly sloping diagonals are not easily seen from the approach, giving the appearance that both the one- and two-story sections of the house float on the land. Punched openings on all sides of the house, often re-emphasized by lighting features, lead the viewer's eye across the composition, linking the component parts of the structure into an integrated whole. This permeable membrane of the structure thus lends visual excitement all within the realm of the mid-century Modern dialect. (LAA)

The large living room, unquestionably the center of the composition, brings together architecture, furnishings, finishes, materials, and lighting into a seamless composition. Working with designer Sarah Hunter Kelly, Edward Loewenstein divided the room into several key areas and worked to provide a comfortable and visually stimulating environment in this central space. On the west side of the room, three long bookshelves mounted on the brick wall bring textural variation and a focus to the seating group just below. Comfortable chairs in eclectic styles and fabrics populate both this seating group and the one nearer the fireplace, dividing the room into entertainment zones. The warm orangey-red color of the brick and the honey-colored, naturally finished wood of the sloping, beamed ceiling bring great warmth to the room, in addition to the fabrics and textures provided by the furniture itself. Light from many sources, both natural and artificial, washes across these surfaces and furnishings, lending a sense of drama and an inviting quality to the living room. The large window-walls of sliding glass doors stand in sharp contrast to the two-sided chimney, a massive brick box that divides the living room from the play room adjacent to the north. Loewenstein deftly "lightens" the visual load of the fireplace in this sharp contrast with the thinness and the permeability of the openings onto the back terrace. (CTB)

Loewenstein sets accordion folding doors (*above left*) next to the brick chimney between the living room and the adjoining playroom, another example of the many ways that the Stern Residence continues to surprise and change as it is experienced by the visitor. In opening and closing the doors, the owners change the viewer perceptions of the flow of space and bring privacy to key areas of the house. Loewenstein implies a long hallway, a central feature in many of his residential compositions, in connecting the dining room to the living room. Rather than encasing a separate space for circulation, it becomes a circulation space through which passes light from both north and south. What would have been a hallway in former commissions dematerializes here, joining the two spaces together in light (*above right*). (PLL)

On the lower floor of the two-story wing, the master bedroom brings to light Loewenstein's interest in dematerialization, as the banks of horizontal windows meet in the corner of the room and connect the owners of the house to the landscape beyond. Just like the sliding doors of the living room and play room, the windows here serve as permeable filters uniting inside to out and softening the crisp geometries of the composition. In the two-story wing, Loewenstein stacks the two bedrooms on each level atop one another, a design decision that likely stems from site constraints. (PLL)

In the adjoining front hall, the sculptural L-shaped "floating" staircase lends a sense of drama to the house. Besides linking the first and second floors together, this architectural element brings together the two levels and supplies a focal point for the front of the house. The openness of the staircase speaks the same language as the large sheets of glass throughout the home, a certain fluidity of light and space as inscribed by architectural elements. The floating stair thus contrasts with the massive masonry block of the fireplace in the living room, an element in which the viewer can see the traditionally solid element of a staircase floating apart into its component pieces, bathed in light. (CTB)

The design team communicates the movable and adjustable nature of the space, sometimes expressed architecturally, more often in light suffusing across surface and sweeping through space. To this task, Edward Loewenstein used the talents of lighting designer Thomas Kelly. The light stacks throughout with layers provided through window and door openings to the exterior while the lighting coffers obscure the fluorescent fixtures and provide a location from which light sweeps across the naturally finished siding and onto the ceiling above. Light changes the understanding of the space and dematerializes the surface materials. (PLL)

Materials lend warmth to and soften the reception of the building into the surrounding landscape. Slate, brick, naturally finished and stained siding, all basic regional building materials, lend an air of quiet rest to the structure. As in his other buildings, built-ins shape the spaces around them. In this instance, the service spaces (not so much the storage spaces) do the work of zoning the house. This minimum of enclosed spaces for bathrooms and the kitchen, and to house the fireplace, hint at the maxim "less is more," repeatedly espoused by design practitioners working in the Modern idiom at mid-century. The sculptural composition that results allows an experience through which the viewer occupies a sculpture of light and form. (PLL)

The square punched skylights within the deep overhang on the rear of the structure suggest a playfulness with light and pattern in the composition. Loewenstein dematerializes the structure of the building to let light dance across the floor surface. (PLL)

Several changes to the floor plan in use demonstrate the flexibility of Loewenstein's designs to changing family needs. In 1963–64, the Stern family converted the carport of the original composition into a recreation room. The heating equipment, moved from the adjoining room, allowed a hallway space to be opened between the recreation room and the rest of the house. The kitchen core remains intact, following its original configuration, including provision for an indoor barbecue and the preservation of the Monel sinkboard. Cabinets divide a small breakfast eating area from the main part of the working kitchen. A maid's room and laundry show provision for live-in servants in this area of the house. (PLL)

EVELYN + JOHN HYMAN RESIDENCE : GREENSBORO (1959)

This residential commission bears the strong imprint of Japanese-inspired design and represents a collaboration between Loewenstein, artist Gregory Ivy, landscape architect Raeford Turner (High Point), and contractor Eugene Gulledge. A Japanese-style pergola covers the front walk on the exterior of the house, and the pergola concept continues as a means of marking the entrance hall on the interior. The pergola from the street entrance to the property suggests a balanced asymmetry along the front walk and marks the front entrance. Bronze doors, one with a decorative knocker, provide a focal point for the composition. Firm documents indicate the total price of the house at $51,705, the cost of lot at $7,200, and the architect's fee of $3,560.40.

In May 1958, Loewenstein wrote a letter about the house to Robert Marin Engelbrecht, editor of Architecture at *Living for Young Homemakers Magazine* (the publication that featured the Commencement House of that same year). He explained: "we are designing a house for John and Evelyn Hyman in Greensboro, NC, which appears to fit the requirements of your "Living-Conditioned" house program. We are in the working drawing stage at this time, and we will send you preliminary prints as soon as possible." Loewenstein added a client description in hopes of catching the editor's attention: "John is Sales Manager of Founders Furniture Company, Pleasant Garden, NC and Evelyn formerly employed by Knoll Associates and has been trained as a professional pianist. They have one child. They are real intellectuals with a feeling for fine and progressive design. They are collectors of paintings, utensils, etc., and in addition they have an excellent piece of property with unusual possibilities."[18]

Evelyn Hyman wrote to Loewenstein from the Hotel Adams in New York City in June 1958, explaining that she would be away longer than she thought and would not be able to participate in the selection of furnishings and finishes as she had hoped: "With each free afternoon, I long to be doing some constructive work, had hoped to see new furniture and fabrics, collecting pictures and samples of the better examples. However, I find I no longer have entry to some of the showrooms like Boris Knoll (open only to the trade). Would it be possible for me to do a study which might be of interest to your design class next year? If so, could you send me a letter of introduction, 'to whom it may concern' allowing me to represent you for this purpose? I'd love doing it . . . and it could prove to be fun not only for the gals but also for your office."[19] Loewenstein replied the next day noting that house was progressing well. In a letter from the next month and in interoffice memos to various employees, Loewenstein tracked the changes in the design and ultimately indicating "everything is perfect with the house according to Hyman."[20]

The pergola stands as a marker for entry into the Hyman Residence and a means to divide the front yard space into outside rooms. The pergola continues into the interior, dividing dining room and living room. From the view inside, diners enjoy the outside view of the landscaped lot. (CTB)

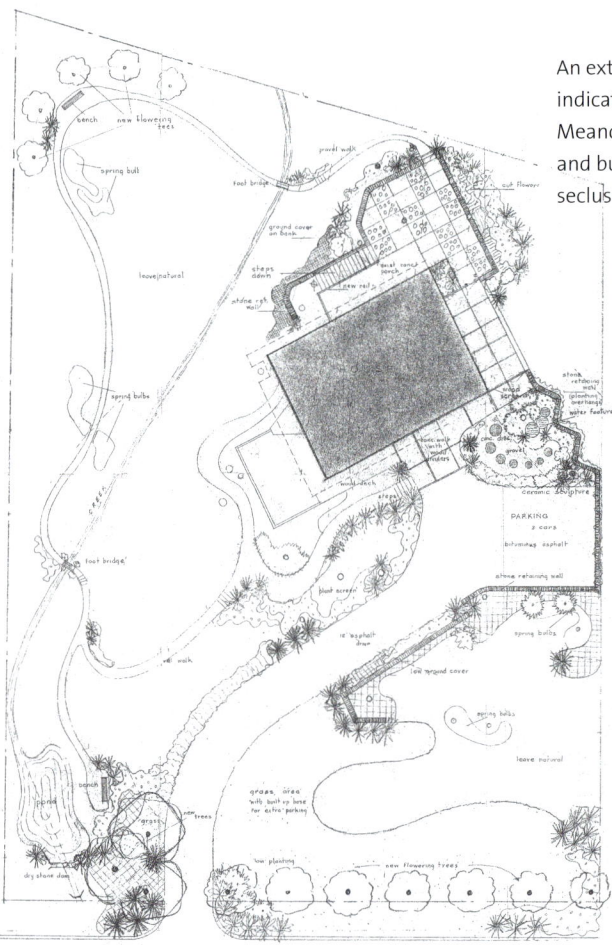

An extensive planting plan, part of the drawing set produced in the studio, indicates the original owner's desire to encase the structure in nature. Meandering paths throughout the site provide views of the floating platforms and butterfly roof. Native plantings and shrubs contribute to the feeling of seclusion within a busy mid-century neighborhood. (LAA)

Further evidence of Loewenstein working with the site can be seen in the details: the notching of the roof on the south façade (*left*) lets nature literally engage with the house, the terracing and levels of the site to take advantage of views to the building and to the very features the owner hoped to preserve, the lacy-like quality of the original deck and its more contemporary counterpart. The fireplace flues copy the form of the nearby tree, grounding the composition (*right*). All of these features help the viewer understand that the simple details of the house give a glimpse into a world where economy of materials and their straightforward arrangement speak to the Modernist sensibility of good design for all. In addition, extensive use of stained siding and fieldstone contribute to the emergent earthy character of the design. Paired with expansive glass windows and the presence of metal, the panoply of forms and textures through the materials represents a visual treat for the eye. (Jennifer René Tate)

California architect Jim Johnson, hired by the current owners in 2007 to design two new decks compatible with the structure, adds to the sensation of the nest like structure with his design intervention. (Jennifer René Tate)

JOANNE SPANGLER RESIDENCE : DANVILLE (1958–1959)

Imagine a client so wrapped up in nature that she desired a house floating in the treetops. Such a commission awaited Edward Loewenstein in Danville, Virginia, for the residence of Joanne Spangler. Loewenstein designed a cantilevered scheme so that the house hovered over the streambed and the deeply wooded slopes below. Grounded by a fieldstone foundation and a triangular plinth in which is embedded the chimney flue, the house played with the soaring nature of the floating planes anchored to the earth. All around, outdoor living spaces contributed to the ethereal experience of this sanctuary nestled in the trees.

Those outside spaces expanded the reach of the house's compact 1,500 square foot plan. As fluid barriers, walls made of large sheets of glass connected the indoors to these outdoor extensions, thus taking advantage of views all around the site. Artfully naturalized plantings further shaped the site architecturally to provide a series of paths and rooms for owner and guest enjoyment. In the quirky nature of the site, a stream running along the base of a steeply-pitched slope, Loewenstein saw an opportunity to make use of a parcel of land undeveloped because of the challenges it presented in terms of both topography and access. He masterfully used the limitations of the site to maximize the impact of the structure.

Like the exterior of the Spangler Residence, Loewenstein took advantage of the stunning views, leaving the occupants to float in the trees while inside the structure. Interlocking interior and exterior experience, Loewenstein placed floor-to-ceiling glass walls around three sides of the main living space that contains both living and dining areas. The fourth side of the space contained the kitchen and bathroom, a solid around which residents and visitors to the home enjoyed the other living spaces, a den and a bedroom, in addition to the great room facing south. The pitch of the butterfly roof that provided so much visual delight on the exterior contributed to the expansive and uplifting space grounded by the central core. Artificial lighting reinforced the sweep of the space as Loewenstein highlighted architectural features and demonstrated an agility at subtleties of materiality as expressed therein. Both wall washes and task lighting helped zone the space into several seating and eating areas. At the south edge of the great room, the fireplace sat within a rock surround, further grounding the composition. Rather than a massive chimney, a simple metal flue rose on the exterior as a vent for this feature and drew the eye skyward without blocking the direct view from the living space.

The front door sits in the middle of the long façade of the structure at the convergence of the butterfly roof. (CTB)

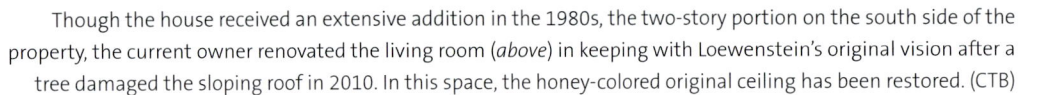

Though the house received an extensive addition in the 1980s, the two-story portion on the south side of the property, the current owner renovated the living room (*above*) in keeping with Loewenstein's original vision after a tree damaged the sloping roof in 2010. In this space, the honey-colored original ceiling has been restored. (CTB)

The living room, dominated by a circular fireplace (also attributed to Ivy), opens to a panoramic view of a Japanese-style garden on the north side of the house, a large open space with a vaulted ceiling supported by steel beams encased in wood. The freestanding flue defines an anchor for the center of the living room around which a curving, linear sofa provides seating for guests. Clerestory lighting opens the view to the wooded lot and allows light to slip into the space. The patio just outside the living room, defined by pergola beams and columns, offers livable outdoor entertaining areas in a garden setting. (CTB)

Pebbled beds substitute for grass, representing the landscape as a Japanese-style garden. Planting materials and rocks underscore the architecture and the treescape in the various sections of the small yard, maximizing views and experience. (CTB)

Extending from a large opening off of the living room, beams cover a patio space that extends the living room outdoors. (*Popular Gardening and Living Outdoors*, Fall/Winter 1967)

Japanese-style gardens surround this structure on its tight suburban lot, each outdoor space essentially shaped by architectural and natural elements to make it a "room." The pierced concrete block walls lend playfulness and privacy to the spaces. The designs for the gardens by landscape architect Raeford Turner were published in *Better Homes and Gardens* in 1966 and *Popular Gardening and Living Outdoors* in 1967. (*Popular Gardening and Living Outdoors*, Fall/Winter 1967)

The current owners' attention to detail in both furnishings and finishes respects the mid-century residence and Loewenstein's frame yet provides a quite livable and up-to-date experience for the twenty-first century. The sloping butterfly roof draws attention to the tree canopy and living spaces outdoors. (CTB)

The overhauled kitchen (*above*) remains in its mid-century configuration, partially open to the adjacent breakfast area. New granite counters replace the original Formica surface and new hardware complements the original cabinets. The skylight in the kitchen, here, and in the adjoining bathroom, provide a connection to nature even in the interior core, not to mention that they serve as handy nightlights in the full moon. (CTB)

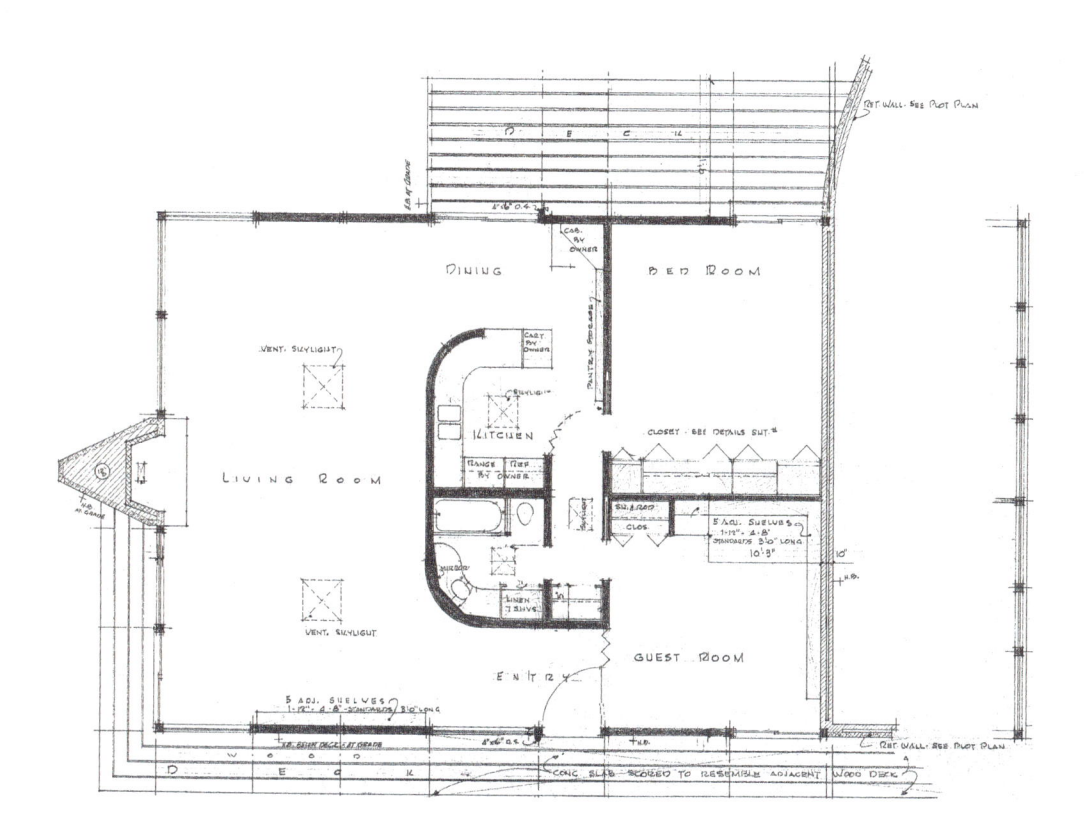

The 1952 floor plan shows the ubiquitous built-ins and ample storage areas that fit in nooks throughout, maximizing the square footage for human occupancy and providing much needed locations to store clothing, dishes, books, and more. In the bedroom, storage bins and closets populate the entire east wall, bringing useful order to the economical floor plan. In the bath, Loewenstein specified similar storage cabinets. Skylights in the kitchen and bathroom provide connections to nature even in the interior core to the structure, not to mention that they serve as handy nightlights in the full moon. (LAA)

Whether in the historic view (*top*) or the current day one (*bottom*), the simple palette of materials — a cork floor, glass walls, a naturally finished wood ceiling, a stone fireplace, large panels of curtains for privacy — provides the setting for comfortable tables and chairs in groups throughout the living space. These materials, transformed as light washes inside, all spring from the region and remind the viewer of the wealth of materials available in the Piedmont deployed by Loewenstein and his firm on such projects. (*top*, from *Town and Country Living*, October 15, 1978; *bottom*, CTB)

JOANNE + WAYNE DAVIS RESIDENCE : PLEASANT GARDEN (1959–1961)

According to John Hyman's business partner, Wayne Davis, the Hymans elected to build a Modern house in Greensboro, while Davis and his family stayed near Founders Furniture Company in Pleasant Garden. Hyman believed that either he or Davis needed to be near the factory if any issue needed to be addressed. The result was while Loewenstein worked on the Greensboro house for the Hymans, he simultaneously designed a spreading two-story house in Pleasant Garden for the Davises. On a 5-acre tract of land, Loewenstein carefully sited the structure, taking advantage of the topography to comfortably settle the building into the environment. Clerestory windows opening into the kitchen and dining room peek above the flat roof of the bedroom wing at the approach to the house. An integrated carport completes the vista, accommodating the automobile within the scheme. When later asked if she had always been comfortable within her Modern home Joanne Davis exclaimed, "I had never been in such a house but, once I experienced the light and the views, I just knew this is how I want to live," referring not just to the physical and tangible elements of her home but rather expressing a way of life, an altered point of view and a positive change inspired by design.[21]

The Davis Residence combines the lessons of several earlier commissions in layout, organizational principles, and siting: the Carter Residence, Loewenstein Residence, and Bertling Residence. At the center of the composition, the fireplace, adjoining storage compartments, and basement steps separate the private bedroom wing from the public rooms, as in the ample use of built-ins to divide space in the Loewenstein house. The carport links directly to a service entrance (and into the kitchen) as well as the main entrance to the residence for visitors, echoing the Carter design. The living room, placed perpindicular to the mass of the house, helps to capture an exterior space. Though the Carter Residence shares a similar configuration, Loewenstein takes advantage of the sloping site to elevate a deck, rather than a patio directly on the surface of the ground, as is more typical of his other designs. Excellent landscape views from this deck and from the rooms facing it on two sides bring the outside and inside into a fluid relationship. The open nature of the rear of the house contrasts the solid walls at the front of the composition, underscored by the placement of the carport that screens the front entrance from view and exposure directly to the street, recalling the Bertling commission.

The clerestory windows from the family room peak over the flat roof planes of the bedroom wing in this driveway view of the Davis Residence. A carport completes the composition, to the left. (PLL)

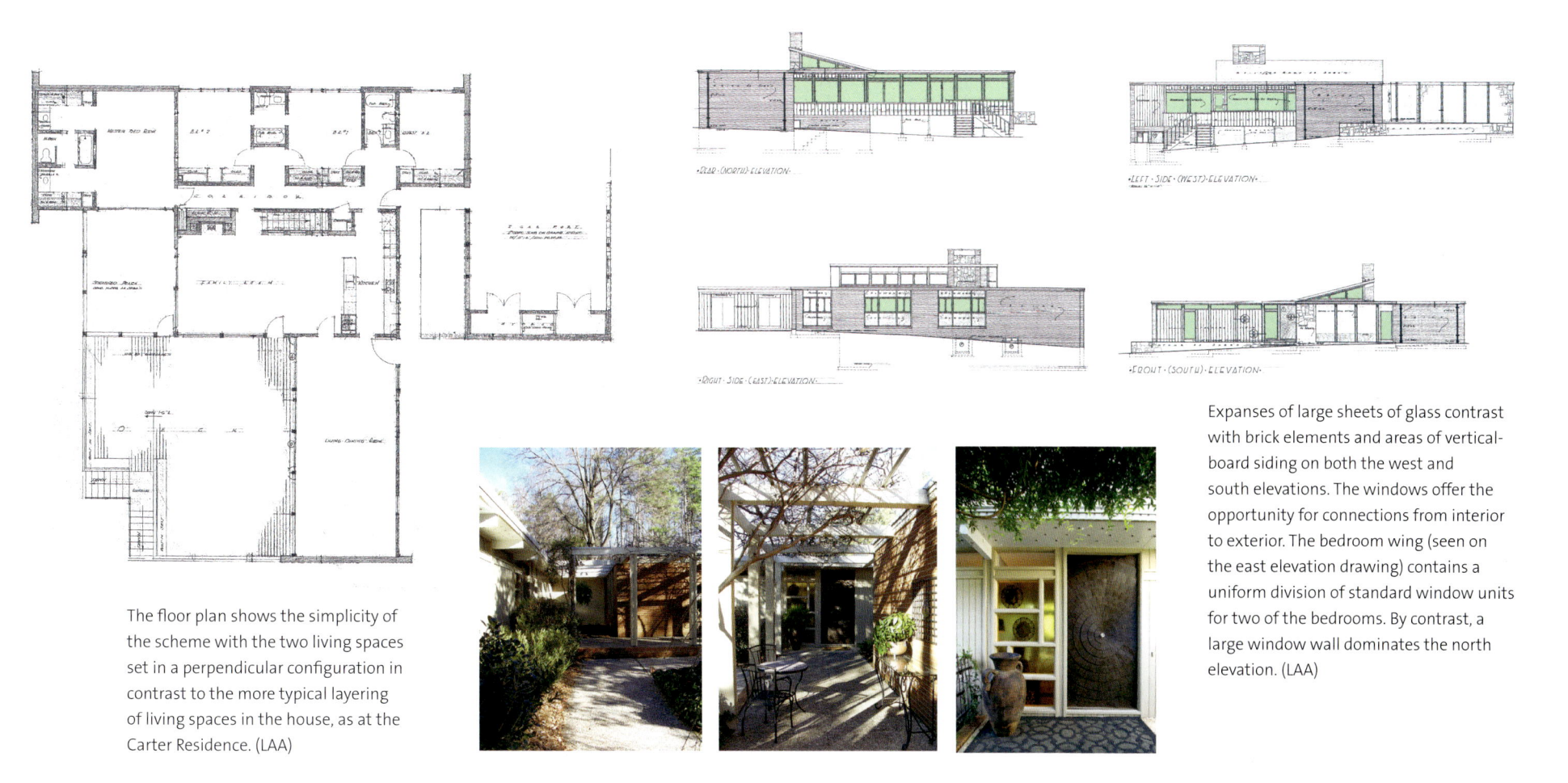

The floor plan shows the simplicity of the scheme with the two living spaces set in a perpendicular configuration in contrast to the more typical layering of living spaces in the house, as at the Carter Residence. (LAA)

Expanses of large sheets of glass contrast with brick elements and areas of vertical-board siding on both the west and south elevations. The windows offer the opportunity for connections from interior to exterior. The bedroom wing (seen on the east elevation drawing) contains a uniform division of standard window units for two of the bedrooms. By contrast, a large window wall dominates the north elevation. (LAA)

At the rear of the garage, a vine-covered pergola provides shelter for the front entry of the house (*left*). This transitional zone shares similarities with the Hyman Residence (1959). Horizontal elements extend from the garage wall (*center*) and the main structure, framing a garden space at the entry for the residence. The metal front door to the structure (*right*) features a central knob next to a colored-glass sidelight. (CTB)

71

Upon entering the structure, a wall of windows opening to the deck beyond frames one side of the expansive living room. The case pieces along the far wall are among many furnishings manufactured at Pleasantville's Founders Furniture Company nearby. (CTB)

The clerestory windows, in both dining room (*above*) and adjoining kitchen (*right*), contribute to the open nature and sense of light in the space. Furnishings and artwork provide textures and colors in this otherwise neutral space. (CTB)

73

In the kitchen (*left*), all of the original cabinets and fixtures still serve the house's residents, as detailed in the drawing (*below*). The compartmentalized bathroom (*right*) shares common vocabulary with Loewenstein's other houses of the 1950s, with ample built-in cabinets to accommodate the users, as is the case with the closets in the bedrooms. The vertical windows were added to the bathroom in view in the 1970s. (*above*, PLL; *below*, LAA)

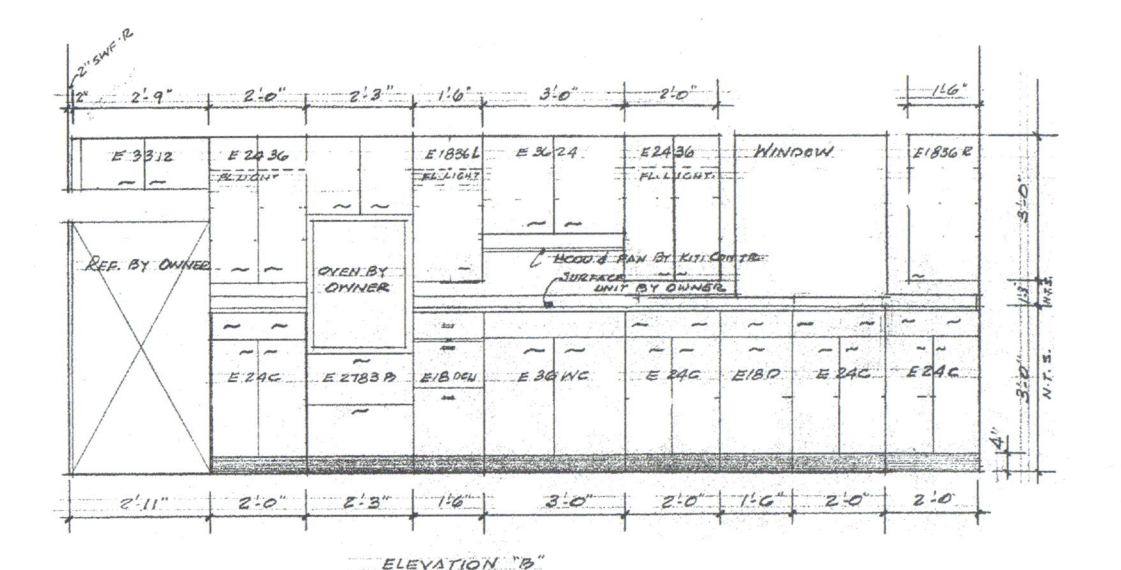

A comparison of the original plan for the east wall elevation of the family room reveals the sensitive interior treatment and detailing in this home, and the connection to Founders Furniture Company. Rather than incorporate the panels and brick as detailed in the drawing (*below*), Wayne and Joanne Davis mounted Founders Furniture case pieces to the wall, bringing their livelihood into their family space. The integration of such elements lent great cohesion to the structure and provided a great example of Loewenstein working with clients to accommodate their belongings. (*above*, PLL; *below*, LAA)

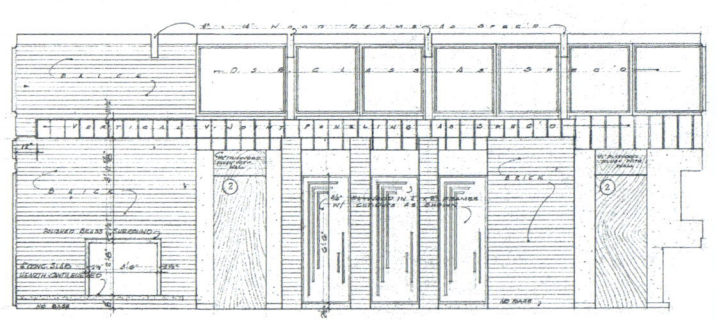

The two-level deck supplies ample living space adjacent to dining room and living room, as well as occupiable space outside the den. Deep overhanging eaves throw strong shadow patterns on this and other façades. Two half-height walls define the two deck levels and provide a means of access for the stairway to the yard. (CTB)

The view from the back deck of the structure reveals the terrace for the swimming pool and site beyond (*top*). The neatly wooded site closes around the structure, locking building and landscape into a mutually supportive relationship, with the pool and the deck layers (*bottom*) building toward the mass of the house. (CTB)

BETTIE S. + ROBERT S. CHANDGIE RESIDENCE : GREENSBORO (1958)

Edward Loewenstein's subtle approach and good client relations won him the commission for the Robert S. and Bettie S. Chandgie Residence. According to Mr. Chandgie, Charles Hartmann Jr. represented the other choice of architect in town, and his "hard and tough ways" convinced the young couple building their first house to select Loewenstein. Mr. Chandgie further reported that Loewenstein worked well in developing the building and its furnishings with Otto Zenke, a New York designer who was then working at Morrison Neese, a downtown department store in Greensboro. Mrs. Chandgie indicated that Zenke had completed some interior design work for other members of her family and thus she was familiar with his work of mixing styles in Modern dwellings: "he was good and up and coming . . . you wanted him if you could get him." Zenke, in working to establish his own design firm and some independence from Morrison Neese, encouraged the Chandgies to place their house on the 1957 Parade of Homes

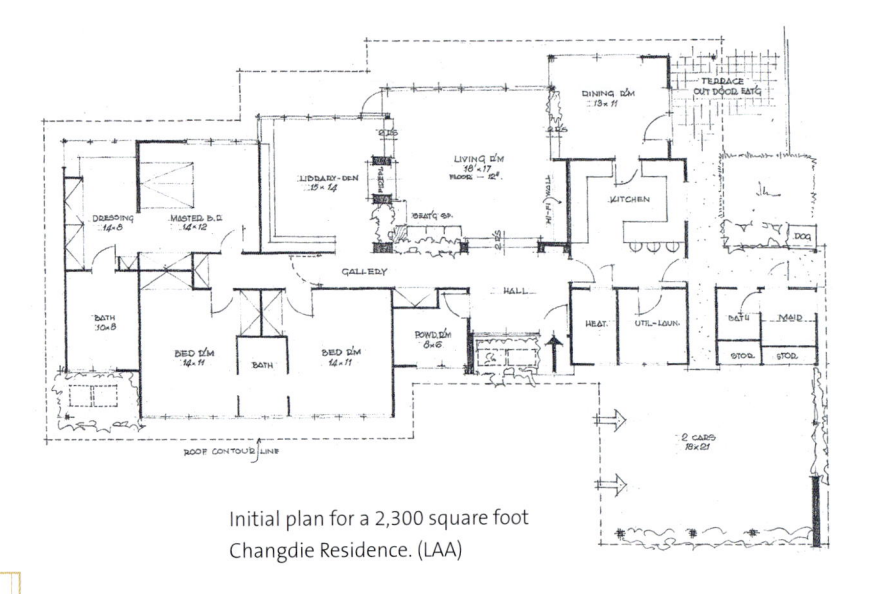

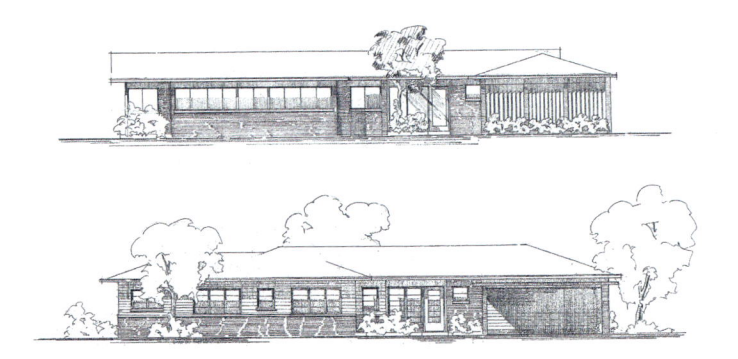

Initial plan for a 2,300 square foot Chandgie Residence. (LAA)

Two alternative front elevations for the original plan. (LAA)

to generate interest in Zenke's approach. Observing a bit of an ego with Zenke, Mr. Chandgie, by contrast, characterized Loewenstein as someone "more cooperative," someone who fit "like an old shoe," someone who, "if he disagreed he did so with good manners."[22] Chandgie credits Zenke with the innovation of curved corners in the dining room. But firm records suggest an alternative. Much design development took place in the early stages, from 1956 until 1957, for this property and the drawings the firm produced in that time period indicated a far bolder vision for the house than what was eventually constructed.

The livable house has served three generations of the family and epitomizes easy living, according to Mrs. Chandgie. The house featured the double-stacked living room and family room present in many Loewenstein schemes. With an off-center front door, visitors entered a foyer between the living room and a dining room with rounded corners, made possible by special bricks manufactured by the Boren Brick Company. An ell reaches from the front of the house to the south, containing the bedrooms and den. The kitchen and service areas of the house, including a maid's room and a carport beyond, open off the dining room and create a U-shaped back of the house.

Design development drawings in the firm archives help us to see the evolution of the house from its earliest stages in 1956 as a relatively conventional Ranch-style house of 2,300 square feet to a more dramatically Modern dwelling of more than 3,400 square feet with low-hanging horizontal planes on the exterior and a curved wall in the dining room. Loewenstein and firm employees offered next a tri-level scheme of 4,795 square feet on four levels, before the clients settled on a final plan in January 1957. All of these drawings demonstrate the conversations between architect and client to arrive at a design solution in keeping with budget and aesthetics.

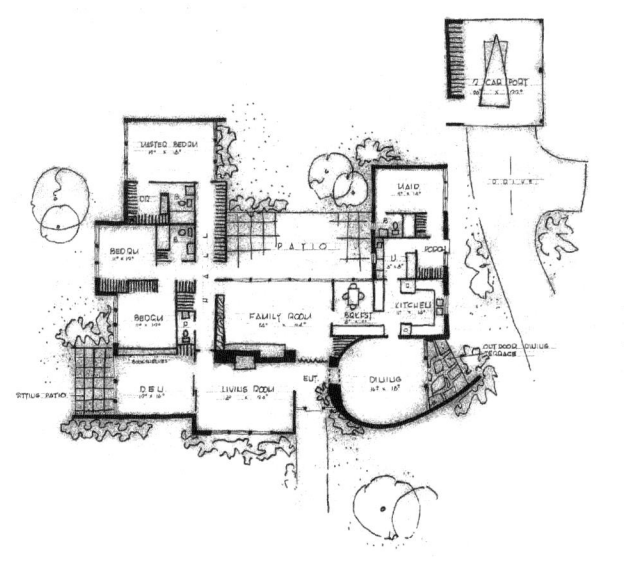

Final front elevation (*top*) and floor plan #2, for a 3,251 square foot house. (LAA)

Elevation proposal for plan #2. (LAA)

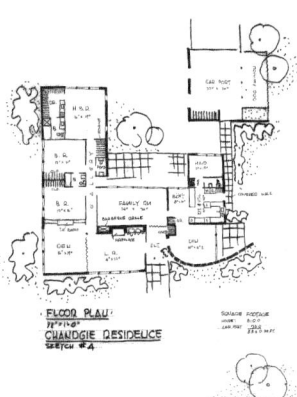

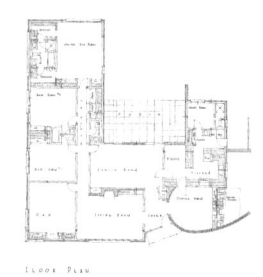

Design development drawings for plan #2. (LAA)

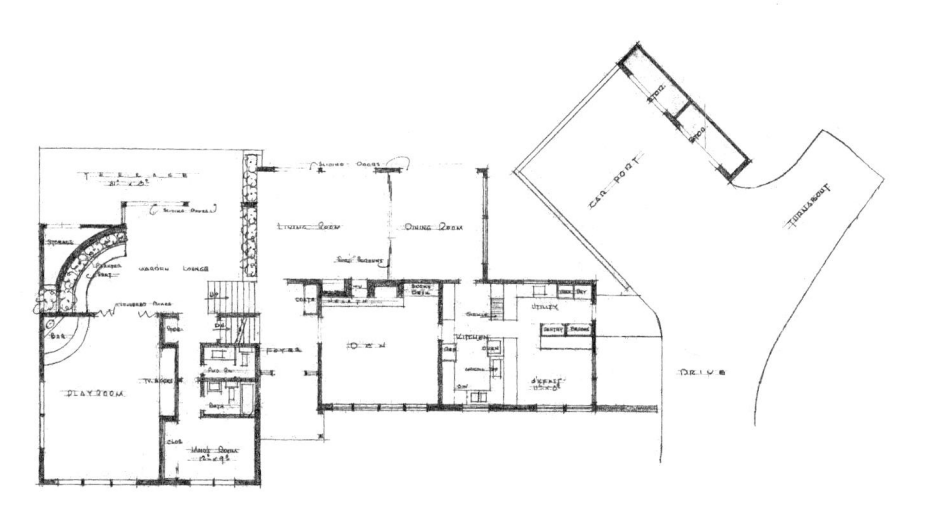

Plan #3, a three-level scheme on four floors, for a total of 4,795 square feet. (LAA)

Elevation alternatives for plan #3. (LAA)

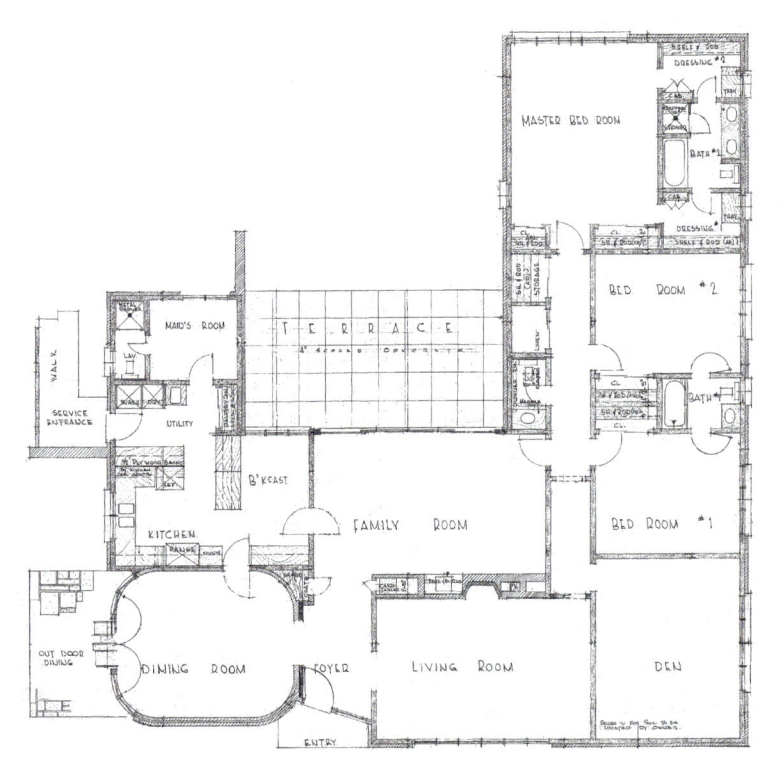

Plan #4. (LAA)

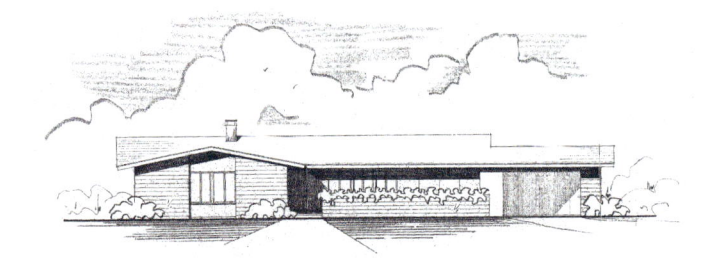

The Changdie Residence, as constructed. (PLL)

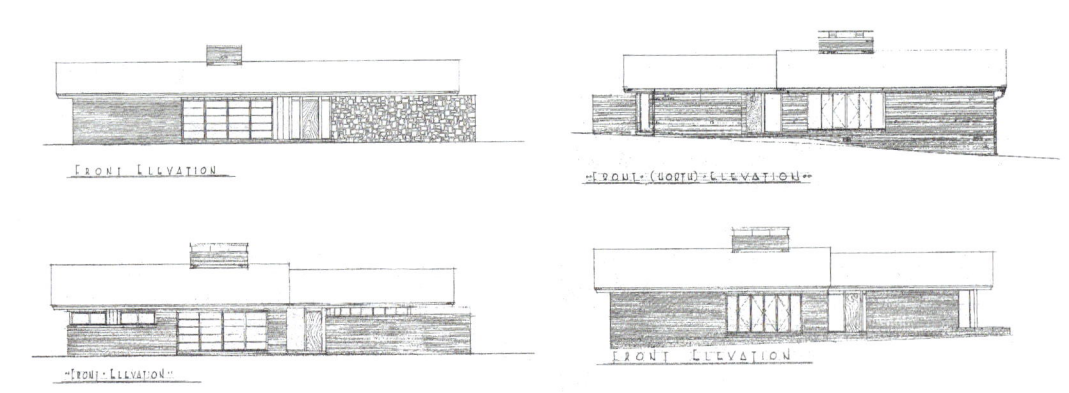

Elevation studies for plan #4. (LAA)

BETTY + CHARLES ROTH RESIDENCE : GREENSBORO (1958)

Following the Chandgie's lead, the Roths engaged Otto Zenke as interior designer, cementing a collaboration between the two design professionals. Toying with the idea of a Modern house, Mrs. Roth thumbed through design magazines to discern the kinds of features that she hoped would be in the residence, and this was not unusual as a design method employed at Loewenstein-Atkinson. What resulted was, according to Mrs. Roth, "a very comfortable place to live, a good house and an easy house."[23]

The residence stood as one point in the social network that Loewenstein accessed through excellent client relations. The Roth family and the Chandgie family, related through marriage, made easy the selection of Loewenstein for both commissions. The Roths, good friends of Joan and Richard Steele, encouraged the couple to retain Loewenstein to design their residence on Woodland Avenue, and they did so in 1964. Charles Roth worked as an attorney in partnership with Herbert Falk, who also retained Loewenstein to design a residence in 1966.

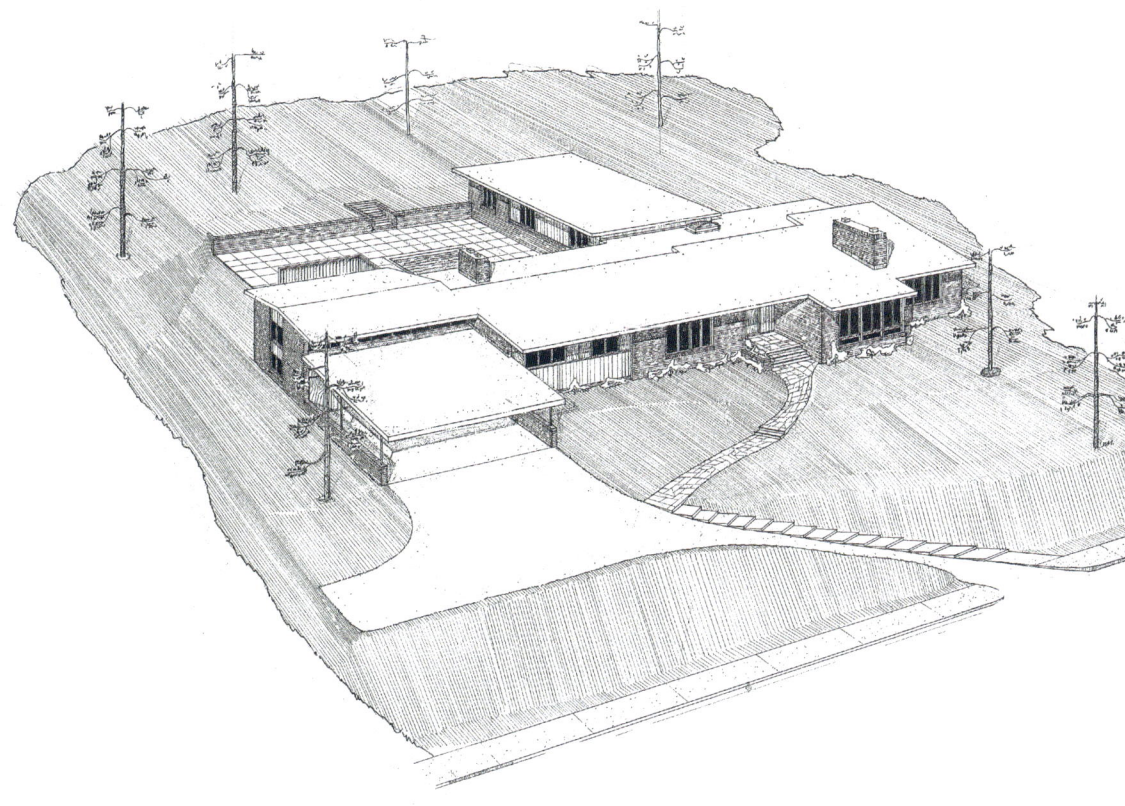

Sited on a steeply sloping lot, the Roth Residence followed a design trajectory not dissimilar from the Chandgie Residence. As a cost-saving measure the clients elected, well into design development, to change the form of the building dramatically with the removal of the clerestory window system and the installation of a gable roof in its place. This axonometric (*above*) shows the building as originally intended by the firm, the photograph (*left*) demonstrates the final outcome of the major design change. (*above*, LAA; *left*, PLL)

notes

1. Roger Clark et al., *School of Design: The Kamphoefner Years*, 1948-1973 (Raleigh, 2007). Henry Leveke Kamphoefner Papers, MC 198, Special Collections Research Center, NC State University Libraries, Raleigh.

2. M. Ruth Little, *The Town and Gown Architecture of Chapel Hill, North Carolina, 1795–1975* (Chapel Hill, NC, 2006). Claudia R. Brown and Diane E. Lea, "A Bastion of Modernism in the Southern Part of Heaven: William Wurster and the Webbs of Chapel Hill," presentation at the 2007 Preservation North Carolina Conference, Raleigh.

3. "Black Mountain College, 1933–57," http://blackmountaincollegeproject.org/History/history2.htm (accessed 12 June 2013).

4. Concord native Arthur Gold (A. G.) Odell Jr. (1913–1988) trained at Duke, Cornell, and the École des Beaux Arts in Paris before beginning work in New York for architect Wallace K. Harrison and industrial designer Raymond Loewy. In 1939, he established a solo practice in Charlotte, designing a handful of Modernist houses in the 1950s alongside those in traditional styles. Eventually the practice grew to well over 50 employees and received a wide range of commissions, including the modern Charlotte Coliseum (1955). Odell was president of AIANC from 1943 to 1954 and became the first national AIA President from North Carolina in 1965. His firm's Wachovia Bank Building opened as the "largest all electric building in the state," and their Burlington Industries Corporate Headquarters, which received recognition by the South Atlantic Regional Council of the American Institute of Architects in 1974 for its design. Wachovia replaced the original gray enamel and blue-tinted window façade of the building with vivid pink tones in the early 1990s, and the structure was reclad again in 2007 with its new condominium use. The Burlington Industries building was imploded in 2005 to make way for a shopping center expansion. Charlotte Landmarks Commission, www.cmhpf.org/S&Rs_20Alphabetical_20Order/surveys&rcoliseum.htm; Triangle Modernist Houses, www.trianglemodernisthouses.com/odell.htm.

5. Established in 1953 by Leon McMinn, Robert Norfleet, and John F. Wicker, this firm served as architects of record for Page High School (1956) and a handful of other public school buildings, Starmount Forest Country Club (1957), Friendly Shopping Center (1958), War Memorial Coliseum and Auditorium (1959), BB&T Tower (1969) in downtown Greensboro, and a host of projects in the state. No information is known about their residential work. J. Hyatt Hammond established a partnership with Jack J. Croft in Asheboro in 1953, with a branch office in Greensboro in 1962. Hyatt bought out Croft and reorganized the firm with a Greensboro address by 1968. In its early history, Croft and Hyatt designed modern houses in Asheboro. In the 1980s and 1990s, Hyatt's firm shaped buildings in Greensboro and continues to do so. The American Institute of Architects 1962 and 1970 Directories, http://communities.aia.org/sites/hdoaa/wiki/Wiki Pages/1962 American Architects Directory.aspx and http://communities.aia.org/sites/hdoaa/wiki/Wiki Pages/1970 American Architects Directory.aspx, respectively; Triangle Modernist Houses, www.trianglemodernisthouses.com/hammond.htm.

6. Circa, Inc., "Historic Resources Survey Planning Phase Report 1940–ca. 1970," prepared for City of Greensboro Department of Housing and Community Development and the NC State Historic Preservation Office (2009).

7. In 1969, Gulledge became Assistant Secretary of the U.S. Department of Housing and Urban Development.

8. Loewenstein wrote to Tasco Motion Picture Productions in 1953, recounting the history of the firm and noting, "Our firm has been staffed with a maximum of 28 people, which sustained branches in Raleigh, Southern Pines, Reidsville, Burlington, and Wilmington, North Carolina, and also Martinsville, Virginia. At the present time we are in a 'republican' frame of mind and we are closing up our branches as fast as we can. The staff has included the average run of people, from brilliant architectural thinkers to morons, religious fanatics to convicts, etc." Loewenstein to Roy W. Marsh, 4 February 1952, Loewenstein-Atkinson Architects firm records, private collection, Greensboro, NC (hereafter LAA).

9. Though not possible to completely reconstruct payroll records, the following names of employees were garnered through an extensive search in the firm records: David J. Arnold, Jerry Bain, James L. Brandt, Bettie Inabinette Briggs, Virginia Bright, Jeannette Brown, Bill Bullington, Ellen Kjsones Cash, William Cofer, Kenneth W. Cogan, Sol William Cohen, Carl D. Coker, Charles J. Doss, James E. Douglass, Cameron Harrison Fair, Henry Faucette, Donald H. Fogleman, Julius Stephan Friedlaender, William T. Galliher, W. C. Gay, Clinton Gravely, William J. Gupple Jr., Sara S. Gwyn, Frank Harmon, William McKinley Harris, Thomas T. Hayes Jr., James S. Helm, Henry P. Henkel, Thomas P. Heritage, Toby Hicks, Irwin J. Hirsch, W. Edward Jenkins, David H. Jurney, Jaroslav Kabatnik, K. Richard Kidd, Beverly P. Kivett, Sherold Paul Klein, Helen M. Levin, Vernon E. Lewis, Robert J. Lysiak, Lawrence Henry Mallard, Enoch Marlow, Thomas F. Marshal, Sandy McKellar, Clyde H. McKinnon, Pattie Mae McMillian, Wilbert Larence Merrick, Willie E, Merritt Jr., W. T. Miskelly, Bill Mitchell, Richard T. Mitchell, Lonnie K. Moore, Lansing Mullis, James S. Neese, R. E. L. Peterson, Isabel K. Parris, Anne Prillaman, James Robert Pugh, Nicholas J. Pyros, Mary E. Rippel, Edwin F. Schnedl, E. M. Shrigley, Gilber McLoud Slack, William Allen Sloan, Blair Leland Smith, Robert E. Smith, Ben L. Spencer, Jane Strickland, John R. Taylor, Mike Troxler, Walter Van Gelder, Henry Grady Walker, Sylvester Wallace, Standford Chester West, Henry Whitfield, Morley Williams, Nathalia Williams, Thomas Wilson, and Walter T. Wilson. In addition, bookkeepers listed some employees by last name only: Browning, Byrum, Gwyn, Inman, Kirkman, Leland, Rottman, Spainhour, Streat, and Yunik.

10. Jim Schlosser, "Dudley Nominated for Historic Status," *Greensboro News & Record*, 3 September 2002.

11. In his own firm, Jenkins's later commissions included institutional or commercial buildings: Cumberland Office Building (1965), Smith's Funeral Services (1967), St. Matthews United Methodist Church (1970), and Greensboro National Bank (1974).

12. AIA, *American Architects Directory* (1970), 343.

13. Gravely's later commissions include the Curtis Residence (1967) and the Trelease Residence (1970), both houses for white families outside of east Greensboro, as well as his own residence, begun in 1975. He also designed the Providence Baptist Church (1967) and the Shiloh Baptist Church (1974) with more innovative forms

Two African-American architects joined Jenkins and Gravely in designing significant residential and commercial buildings in Greensboro during the latter half of the twentieth century. Gerard E. Gray (1919–2001) attended North Carolina A&T State University and graduated in 1942 with a degree in architectural engineering, earning a master's degree in the same subject from the University of Illinois in 1949. He returned to Greensboro, serving as both an Associate Professor at A&T and as a draftsman for Greensboro architect and engineer Thomas P. Heritage, who had started his own practice after having worked for Loewenstein. In the 1950s and 1960s, Gray designed modernist split-level and ranch-style residences for prominent members of the black community, including the Melvin Alexander Residence (1961), Dr. Alvin V. Blount Residence (1964), Dr. Charles Fountain Residence (1968), Dr. Eugene Marrow Residence (1968), and the Joe and Eunice Dudley Residence (1972), nearly all members of the A&T faculty. William Streat (1920–1994), who served in 1949 as chair of the architectural engineering department at A&T, trained at the Hampton Institute in Virginia and the University of Illinois before obtaining an M.S. in Architectural Engineering from MIT in 1949, where he met Edward Loewenstein. He worked for the Loewenstein firm as a consultant from 1950 to 1952 and earned registration as the second African-American architect in North Carolina. Hazel Ruth Edwards, "Gaston Alonzo Edwards (1875–1943)," *African American Architects: A Biographical Dictionary*, 1865–1946, ed. Dreck Spurlock Wilson (New York, 2004), p. 136. Streat's residential commissions include the Dr. William Reed Residence (1959), William Streat Residence (1962), Dr. Flotilla Watkins Residence (1963), Dr. Gladys White Residence (1965), Dr. Frank H. White Residence (1965), and Dr. Clarence L. Cokely Residence (1968), some for members of the A&T faculty and others for prominent African-American physicians. Sally Shader, "Modernist Designs from Greensboro's East Side: How Four African American Architects Helped Create a Progressive Postwar Landscape," unpublished paper, UNC Greensboro, 2012.

15 Jane Levy interview with Ellen Kjsones Cash, May 2013.

16 E-mail correspondence, Anne Greene to Patrick Lee Lucas, October 2007.

17 Patrick Lee Lucas, "Sarah Hunter Kelly: Designing the House of Good Taste," *Interiors: Design, Architecture, Culture* 1.1 (2010): 75-90.

18 Loewenstein to Engelbrecht, 6 May 1958, (LAA).

19 Evelyn Hyman to Loewenstein, 8 June 1958, (LAA).

20 Interoffice memorandum, 19 July 1958, (LAA).

21 Interview with Joanne Davis by Mira Eng-Getz, April 2010.

22 Interview with Robert and Bettie Chandgie, 3 March 2010.

23 Interview with Betty Roth, 9 March 2010.

an experiment in design education

In 1957, Loewenstein began teaching an innovative course in architectural design at Woman's College of the University of North Carolina in Greensboro. Twenty-three students took the year-long course offered through Gregory Ivy's Department of Art, open to both home economics and art majors. According to Ivy, the design-build studio gave "students a real working knowledge of the problems they would face in making homes for themselves and their families." Students achieved working knowledge of design as many opportunities and problems arose, such as a design based on load-bearing construction, material qualities, and, most interestingly, the challenges posed by state-of-the-art technology such as dishwashers, garbage disposals, and aluminum wiring, which cut down wiring cost for the project by over 20%.[1] In Loewenstein's studio class, the students designed a house, oversaw its construction, and decorated the resulting structure, dubbed the "Commencement House" by the college's public relations office.

Acclaim for the structure came from local and national sources. The *Greensboro Daily News* proclaimed the house "as modern as tomorrow," hailing the women who designed it as pioneers, reporting that "they are the first pupils outside the schools of architecture to attempt the complete designing and building of a house." Mereb Mossman, Dean of Instruction at Woman's College, described the project as "an exciting experience in construction," suggesting that the walls of a college building are no longer the boundary lines for a program of learning." Chancellor Gordon W. Blackwell declared that building the house "marks another national 'first' for the college."[2]

At its May 1958 dedication, an event covered by the paper and broadcast on WUNC-TV, North Carolina First Lady Mrs. Luther Hodges, herself an alumna of Woman's College, cut the ribbon on the house. The transcript of the live remote broadcast suggests that all of the students were involved in every aspect of the design, from overall planning to site selection and landscaping, public relations and material donations, the design of the interiors, and the selection of the furnishings and finishes.

Both the *Greensboro Daily News* and *Raleigh News and Observer* covered the opening of the 1958 Commencement House, though no newspaper seems to have carried a similar story for the following two houses. The local press reported, "The choice of color, the natural wood finishes, the brick walls, and the wide glass panels blend the house perfectly with its wooded setting."[3] *McCall's Magazine* explained the design process as one where students divided into committees to research various areas of specialty looking at studies on living and energy patterns. They organized the house around a series of activity centers, planned for specific family needs, and furnished the house in what the students called "warm modern," with an emphasis on interesting textures and

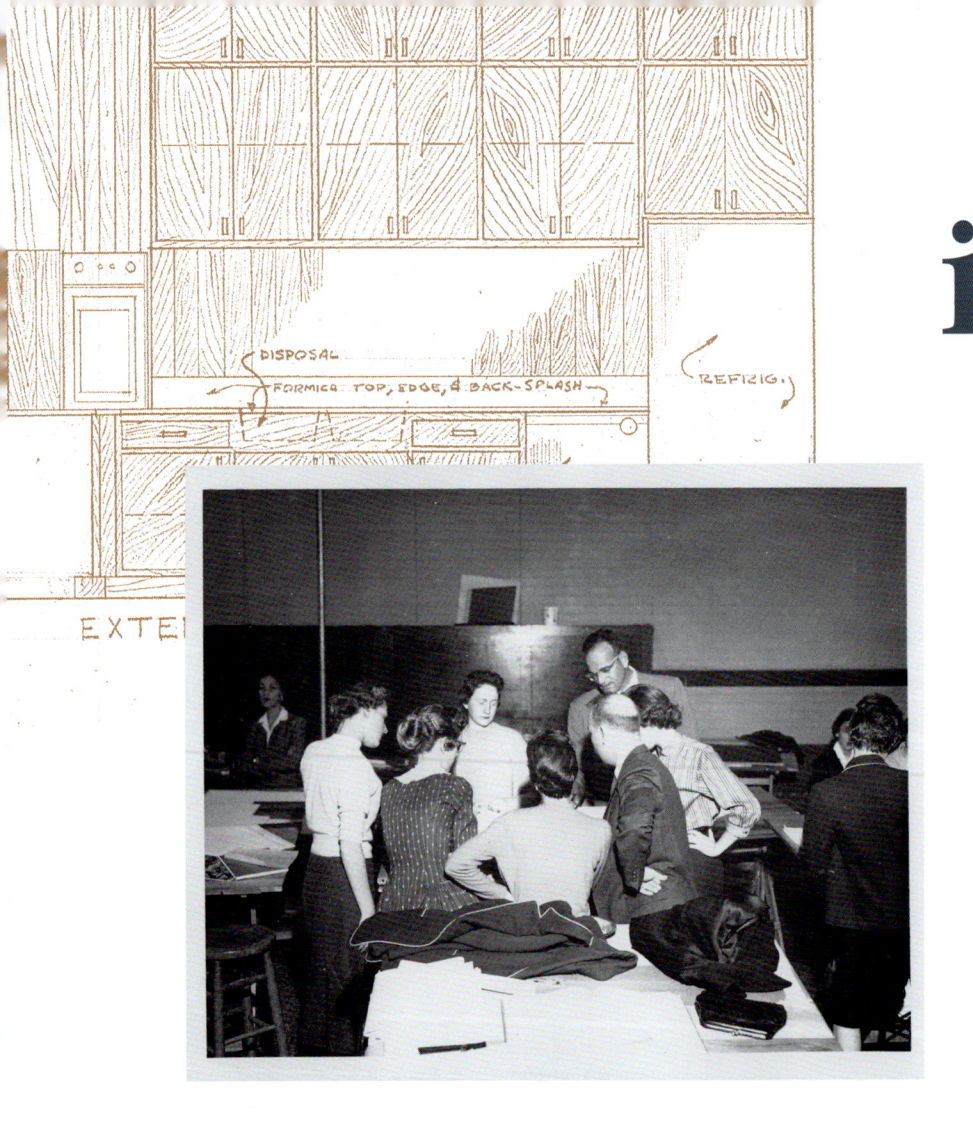

At the Woman's College studio, Edward Loewenstein (rear) gathers with Gregory Ivy (foreground, facing away from camera) and a group of students to discuss design progress on the 1958 Commencement House. (UNCG-SCA)

a blending of interior and exterior finishing materials. *McCall's* described the result of their efforts as a "real honey of a home."[4]

In explaining the motivation of the course, *Southern Appliances Magazine* noted that Loewenstein himself "felt that there was a lack of interest in platform lecturing and that the students needed something to spark their interest," visualizing that if they could "design something and see it carried out in the form of an actual home," they would "have a feeling of solid creativeness," an idea they went after "tooth and nail." Loewenstein and the house's contractor, Eugene Gulledge (Superior Contracting Company of Greensboro), placed two restrictions on the students as they designed: the first relating to the number of people to live in the house, and the second to design a house that could sell in Greensboro. According to Gulledge, "while the house should contain pioneering ideas of layout and design, it should not be so radical as to make it unmarketable."[5]

To build and furnish the house, students cemented partnerships with local building supply companies and house furnishing concerns and utilities, including Duke Power Company, which awarded the house a gold medallion for electrical excellence; Walker-Martin, Inc. (Greensboro), who provided General Electric kitchen and laundry equipment; Southard Electric Company (Stokesdale), the electrical contractor; Appliance and TV Center, Inc. (Greensboro), who donated television sets, a refrigerator, and freezer; Hardware Distributors Company (Greensboro), who provided hardware throughout the house; Dick and Kirkman Heating Company (Greensboro), heating contractors; Dixie Furniture Company (Lexington) and Summit Furniture Company (Greensboro) who provided furniture and case goods, lamps, and accessories.

Though built on speculation (Gulledge and his wife acted as the clients for the students) with a budget of $30,000, the house sold to the Squires family for $45,000 less than two months later. And before that contract was signed, at the dedication of the first house, Ivy and Loewenstein conceived of a second project, continuing to work in partnership with Superior Contracting.

"The only real drawback in this venture," agreed Ivy and Gulledge, "is that we didn't start in time. Ten weeks ago, this was a vacant lot. We expect to overcome that handicap in the future."[6] Loewenstein, Ivy, and Gulledge continued in partnership and achieved their goal for a house built the next year, less than a mile to the west. For a third house, built in 1965 in nearby Sedgefield, they collapsed the design and build process into one semester.

Located on Rockford Road in Irving Park, the 1959 Commencement House had a slightly more modest budget at $24,000 but was still built on speculation, with Gulledge covering the cost of construction until the house sold, to the family of Kenneth Hinsdale, a vice-president for the Jefferson Pilot Insurance Company. The students divided the small, family-oriented, one-story house into public and private zones, orienting the public but cozy dining room and theatrical living room, with its expansive glass wall, toward the wooded lot and a lake view. The private part of the house, for quiet and personal retreat, included three bedrooms and two and one-half baths, as well as ample storage and a dressing room in the master suite. According to the aims of the course, students considered areas zoned for family activity, a step-saving traffic pattern, visual spaciousness beyond actual square footage, easy maintenance, dramatic lighting, and climate conditioning (through a central attic fan and well-placed window and door openings).

As with the previous project, the 1959 Commencement House students sought support from the local community by way of donations and through help from several contractors: electric appliances from Jackson Plumbing, Beamans, Inc., and Appliances and TV Center; furniture from Founders Furniture Company and Thayer-Coggin; lighting fixtures from Prescolite and Lightolier; and assistance from Thomas Electrical Contractors, Inc., Jackson Plumbing, Roberts Tile Company (Sanford); and Huttig Sash and Door (Charlotte). Duke Power company rated the structure a "Gold Medallion Home," the same award as given the 1958 Commencement House.[7] Walter J. Moran served as interior designer for the project, with Loewenstein coordinating student efforts in the studio and on site.

Why there was a six-year hiatus between the 1959 and 1965 Commencement Houses is debatable, but one reason could be due to turmoil in the Department of Art at the Woman's College which resulted in Ivy's departure.[8] Perhaps Gulledge could not afford to bankroll the effort, or maybe the trio of leaders on the first two houses could not find a site suitable for the endeavor. Certainly it was not for the lack of a client. Nancy Downs, the hostess for the WUNC-TV show *Potpourri* that had featured the 1958 Commencement House, expressed interest to Loewenstein suggesting that if he would ever need a client that he should think of her. In the meantime, she had married Herbert Smith and they had started a family. Her desire to serve as the client for the Woman's College design class remained firm, however, and the students once again had the opportunity to work with clients in shaping a "real world" design experience, but this one

continued, page 90

The present owner of the 1959 Commencement House updated finishes and furnishings with an eye toward the original intentions of the students and a twenty-first century interpretation of mid-century modern design he introduced. The playful furnishings in bright citron accent the monochromatic scheme of the living and dining rooms, filled with contemporary art and furnishings. His design decisions preserve the original design intentions of the home, connecting indoors and out through the light wall connecting to the back yard and terrace. (CTB)

MARION + KENNETH P. HINSDALE RESIDENCE : GREENSBORO (1959)

Students prepared this card for distribution to those who visited the house. (Private collection)

The simple entry hall (*left*) sets the stage for the dramatic living room views, with the living room two steps below both entry and dining areas (*center*), the separate levels permitting a borrowing and lending of space and light, with each area maintaining an independence from the others. The devised lighting unifies the formal spaces, alongside a family dining and activity center (*right*) open to the kitchen. In furnishing the house, the students wove texture and color to create a restful setting, easy to maintain. In the original scheme, natural red brick walls provided the backdrop for large art in the dining room, while a massive chimney (also of natural brick) divides living room from kitchen. Richly grained walnut furniture, upholstered in black, brown, and cream imparted an interplay of textures for the rooms, underscored by layered textiles on the curtain wall uniting the two public spaces. The kitchen contained an indoor barbecue as a supplementary cooking area, a generous supply of work counters and cabinets, and efficient undercounter and general overhead illumination. (Jax Harmon)

The front (*top left*) and rear (*top right*) façades of the 1959 Commencement House reveal the design intentions of the class to take advantage of the lake views from the back of the house while minimizing fenestration on the front. The carport, to the right, further separates the house from the street visually through the use of open concrete masonry units used as a screening wall. The two-level terrace in the rear shapes use of the patio into two areas. The large sliding door and open windows bridge inside/out into the living/dining room space beyond. In the present-day view (*below*), the current owner shifted the landscape to include a greater variety of textures, including the installation of a green roof above the carport (*above*: PLL; *below*: CTB)

FRANCES + IRVIN SQUIRES RESIDENCE : GREENSBORO (1958)

Built near the intersection of North Elm Street and Cornwallis Drive on a 95' x 200' wooded lot, the tri-level design of the 1958 house suited the naturally hilly site, with the ground floor opening to the rear of the site, the middle floor providing the entrance at the front, and the top floor taking advantage of views into the wooded lot from a balcony across the back of the structure.

One entered the house through a foyer with a hallway connecting to two bedrooms off to the left, a flight of steps leading to the living room directly ahead, and another flight leading to the dining room below to the right. Many of the rooms took advantage of the great views to the wooded lot and the rear of the house. High peaked ceilings with exposed beams, the open arrangement of the interconnecting rooms, and the rear glass wall combined to give a feeling of spaciousness, while the woodsy tones of browns, grays, and golds dominated the interior and settled the building into its arboreal landscape. (*photos:* UNCG-SCA)

The completion of the first house merited acclaim on the airwaves in one of Greensboro's first live remote broadcasts by WUNC-TV on the *Potpourri* program, hosted by Nancy Downs (later owner of the third Commencement House). Though the tape does not survive from this program, a written transcript suggests that women building a house was big news in 1958. (UNCG-SCA)

The notoriety of the 1958 Commencement House spread from Greensboro to the national press in *McCall's* Magazine, demonstrating the appeal of such an innovative project to audiences far beyond the Greensboro community.

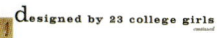

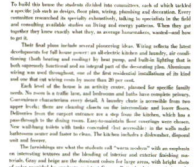

85

This 2008 view of the home shows the two later additions. The room to the left side on the front of the structure and the carport at the far left. (PLL)

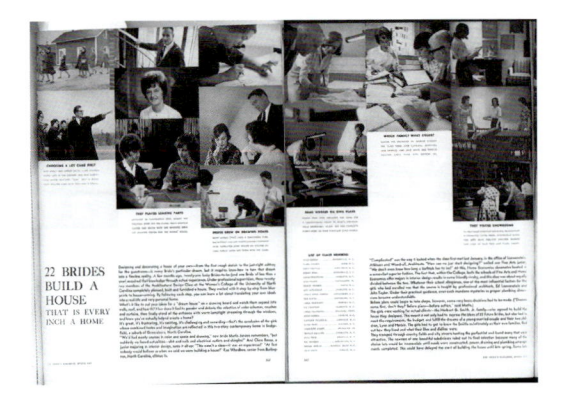

The *Bride's Magazine* spread on the 1965 Commencement House shows members of the class, Loewenstein, and others in various stages of the design process. Indicative of the times and the periodical source, the article profiles each of the class members and their contributions to the project, emphasizing the fact that all were young women of marrying age. (*Bride's Magazine*)

These three views show the interiors shortly before the open house to the public. In the living room (*above*), the master bedroom (*above right*) and the dining room (*bottom right*) and all incorporate a wide variety of textures and lighting effetcs. Each room provides the setting for cleaned line modern furniture of the twentieth century. (Private collection, Wilmington, NC)

NANCY + HERBERT SMITH RESIDENCE : SEDGEFIELD (1965)

The two-story stair (*left*) makes for a dramatic entrance. The nighttime view (*above*) shows how the lighting systems designed by the students affect the formal qualities of the composition. (Private collection)

continued from page 83

Twenty members of the Commencement House studio pose at the groundbreaking in 1958. (UNCG-SCA)

with an incredibly tight time line for completion — one semester to design *and* build.

The students started with a client with very certain ideas about the house. Based on what she learned in her two-year stint as hostess for *Potpourri*, Nancy Smith had done lots of thinking about the house of her dreams: "I love an open kitchen so I can see what's going on . . . I love the feeling of rooms that flow into each other. . . . Most of the time we entertain very informally — just friends, one or two couples dropping over, but three or four times a year, on special days like Derby Day and the Bowl Games, we have twelve to eighteen people in for a buffet. . . . Separateness is important. Herb and I really love our children, but we don't do very well all under each other's feet."[9] These design suggestions from the clients elicited great creativity from the students of the class, with every student submitting a design for consideration by Loewenstein, designer John Taylor, interior consultant Gregory Ivy, and the clients. The winning scheme, a clean-lined two-story proposal by Polly Colville, featured a dramatic 17-foot-high window wall in the entrance hall and a second-floor deck above a terrace overlooking the golf course at the rear of the lot.

Once the house design had been approved, as with the 1958 and 1959 houses, the class divided into committees and evolved detailed plans for living and sleeping areas, kitchen and laundry, as well as site and landscaping. Some students constructed scale models of Colville's design; others put together public relations materials for the house's grand opening. All of the women worked to provide a seamless quality between interior and exterior of the structure through materials — paneling, tile, flooring, and wall covering, many materials left in a natural state.

According to *Bride's Magazine*, class members "were determined that the décor should be an integral part of the house itself, and not superimposed 'like a mink stole over a tennis dress,' " noting that their goal of quiet neutrals in the permanent interior scheme "allowed brilliant, rich colors in paintings, accessories, and upholstery."[10] With budget in mind, the students worked diligently alongside client, contractor, design professionals at school and beyond, and with Loewenstein himself, to complete the enormous task of building a house in three months from the ground up.

All three of the Commencement Houses resulted from innovation espoused by Loewenstein, alongside the students, and the various partners and collaborators who made the efforts possible: Gregory Ivy, first as chairman of the Art Department then as interior designer for the firm; Walter Moran and John Taylor, who assisted Loewenstein in studio on campus and on the jobsite; and Eugene Gulledge, contractor for all three structures. Notably, Gulledge fronted the money for these houses built essentially on speculation, ensuring their market success. The houses also represented the resiliency of Loewenstein, and the firm, to incorporate alternative approaches to the design process in a time of mercurial change for the community and the nation. Just as these houses represented a nonconformity in doing things in an innovative way, and in sitting quietly in the neighborhood settings, so too did students sit in as a form of silent protest in downtown Greensboro in 1960.

notes

1 "Designed by 23 College Girls," *McCall's*, November 1958, 139.

2 *Greensboro Daily News*, 30 May 1958, B2.

3 Ibid.

4 "Designed by 23 College Girls," *McCall's*, November 1958.

5 "Greensboro LBE House Designed by WCUNC Class," *Southern Appliances Magazine*, September 1958, 6–8.

6 Ibid.

7 "A House with a College Diploma," *Living for Young Homemakers* (October 1959) 178-81, 183, 186-87.

8 Will South, *Gregory D. Ivy: Making Greensboro Modern* (Greensboro, NC, 2005).

9 "22 Brides Build a House: That Is Every Inch a Home," *Brides Magazine*, Spring 1965, 163.

10 Ibid., 206.

emerging civilities + situations

as the firm of Loewenstein-Atkinson entered its second decade, its emphasis on producing plans for single-family houses waned. Echoing a general trend in architecture and design work, the realities of investment in staff time to deal with the intricacies of a residential commission did not pay off for the firm. Moreover, Loewenstein encountered more difficult clients who withdrew at various stages of the design development process. Loewenstein, in a letter to his attorney seeking advice on an unfulfilled Danville commission, lamented, "I hope this is our next to last house job. Our last housing job under construction is the Ethridge's, which is about to kill all of us."[1] The second commission followed the pattern of the Spangler Residence, where the owner took the firm's design development plans and shared them with a general contractor, who amended them and brought the cost, size, and detailing of the house more in line with her budget. In the same letter for advice on handling the second commission, Loewenstein wrote, "I know that the plans and drawings were the basis for at least starting the revision on the house and it greatly resembles in every respect what we had drawn." Ultimately, the firm retained an attorney in Virginia who settled the case, with an award of $15,000 to the firm, less $1,200 in legal fees. In Greensboro, a similar case involved a faculty member at Woman's College who had retained the firm to design a small house, involving an honors student from Loewenstein's studio. The client aborted the house plans when she learned of a highway expansion near the plot of land she had selected. The firm was left with no way to charge the client for the plans. The pattern in the firm records indicates that such practice was happening more and more with clients beginning the design process but not completing it. Despite these challenges, Loewenstein successfully completed a handful of commissions reflecting new design ideas or the use of new materials in the 1960s. In a time of enormous change for Greensboro and the nation, these last residential commissions reveal emerging situations that ultimately affected Loewenstein and the firm.

Financial records indicate that the firm operated a significant deficit in 1952, 1954, and 1958, with slim margins of profit in the intervening years. The firm again experienced losses in 1963 and 1964 but maintained profitability otherwise. The deficit situations in the 1950s related to overextension through the development of satellite offices. Jettisoned as an operations model by the 1960s, the firm added partners and changed design focus in part to address the financial situation. In October 1962, Loewenstein and Atkinson struck a letter for a trial partnership with Greensboro architect, Albert C. Woodroof, though no other firm records indicate that any business relationship ever evolved from the the agreement. As early as 1963, firm records suggest that Loewenstein and Atkinson sought other, more viable business models. On 26 July 1967, Virginia Bright sent a notice to the *Greensboro News and Record* recording a name change for the partnership from Loewenstein-Atkinson Architects to Loewenstein-Atkinson-Wilson, Architects and Engineers, noting that W. T. "Tom" Wilson had joined the firm. Though structural, mechanical, and electrical engineers had been present throughout the firm's history, this public shift to a joint architecture-engineering model was reflected in the list of commissions from the 1960s, including the **Archer Elementary School** (1962), **Evergreens Retirement Home** (1963-65), **Greensboro Public Library** (1963-1964), **Golden Gate Shopping Center** (1965), **Greensboro YWCA** (ca. 1965), **Southern Optical Company** (1966–67), and the **Ben L. Smith High School Auditorium** (1969–70) in Greensboro, continued work for **Bennett College**, the **Beth Israel Synagogue** in Fayetteville (1962), and numerous shopping centers in North Carolina, South Carolina, Virginia, and West Virginia. As he had several times in the 1950s, Loewenstein wrote to architectural photographer, Joseph W. Molitor, indicating the ennui of the firm: "We are ready to yell 'uncle.' We have had a siege of really bum work done since our parting of the ways with you some time ago, and I would appreciate your letting me know when you are going to be in Greensboro again, so that we can renew our relations with you."[2] In March of that year, Gregory Ivy replied to Molitor's request to photograph three projects the firm thought to be its best: **Archer Elementary School** (Greensboro); **Beth Israel Synagogue** (Fayetteville); and **Jackson Buff Corporation** (Conover).[3]

Just as the firm experienced a transformation of identity, Edward Loewenstein seemed to be seeking a variety of other outlets for his creative activity and community work. With his involvement at Woman's College in the 1958 and 1959 Commencement Houses, Loewenstein contributed to the education of young designers. He continued to teach an architectural history course there until 1970 and, in 1965, returned to the design studio for the final Commencement House in Sedgefield. Maintaining his advocacy for women, Loewenstein spoke at the 1965 inaugural banquet of the Greensboro Chapter of Women in Construction. That same year, he wrote to Gilbert Carpenter, then chairman of the Department of Art at the University of North Carolina at Greensboro (UNCG) to suggest a change in commitment to teaching: "I have talked to John Taylor about our handling the drawing course the latter part of next year, but from what we can see now, it would be very difficult. We are swamped with work and have lost a great deal on our teaching activities. I must really calm down somewhere and this appears to be the first place. If the situation becomes desperate and you can not get anyone, please do not hesitate to call and we will try to work something out."[4] Loewenstein still maintained intern positions for students from UNCG as well as those from around the world, including several students who had studied at the Sorbonne but gained practical experience in Greensboro.

World travels took Loewenstein and his family to various spots in Europe in the 1960s, including a visit to the ruins of Pompeii in October 1961 and a major journey to France, Spain, and Italy in 1968.[5] Correspondence in the intervening years indicates Loewenstein's interest in making connections to open a European office or at least attaining commissions there. Despite these failed attempts to lure clients to build overseas, Loewenstein wrote to the U.S. Department of Agriculture, the U.S. Department of Commerce, and the Ghana Housing Cooperative to establish an office in Africa. In May 1961, Loewenstein wrote, "We have been wondering if it would be advantageous for us to set up branch operations in one of the new West African nations. Since 1946 we have had a very strong group of Negro architects with us. At the present time, two of them have obtained North Carolina licenses, which is quite unusual, and one of the licensed men is still with us (the other is the head of the architecture department at A&T in Greensboro)." Loewenstein also suggested internships for African students and connections between his firm and an architecture school in Liberia as alternatives. W. K. Mensah of the Ghana National Contractors Association replied in July 1961 that he encouraged Loewenstein moving forward with establishing a branch office in Ghana.[6] The Ghanaian government was less enthusiastic, turning down the proposal that same month.[7]

In December 1964, Loewenstein petitioned the University of Virginia School of Architecture for a position as a student in their graduate program in architectural history. In his letter, he noted his part-time faculty status in the UNCG Department of Art teaching the survey of architecture course and his travel in England, France, Italy, Greece, and Spain, explaining further that he "attended the 21 day course in Vicenza at the International School of Palladian Studies, and I've been trying to find similar, short courses in other countries." Though he did not identify the institution, Loewenstein explained that he was currently taking a course in fallout shelter analysis that would be complete in 1965. He also spoke of his health concerns, indicating, "I've only had one mild heart attack (in 1961) in my 51 years, and I think I could find time to do the work if I could start it after about September of 1965."[8]

A little less than five years later, Edward Loewenstein suffered a second and fatal heart attack at home and died in 1970. He left behind a firm still struggling with its identity as a design concern in Greensboro. Robert Atkinson died a year after Loewenstein, also of a heart attack, leaving the young Tom Wilson to find a suitable partner. He did so in 1971 in collaborating with Robert J. Lysiak — already in employ with Loewenstein, Atkinson, and Wilson. Together they formed Wilson-Lysiak, an engineering firm that continues in practice today.

ALF HOLLAR RESIDENCE (HORIZON HOUSE) : GREENSBORO (1962)

Contractor Eugene Gulledge invited Loewenstein-Atkinson to enter the Alf Hollar Residence in the Horizon House Competition for the design of a structure that focused on the innovative use of concrete. Carolina Quality Block Construction served as the local sponsor for the nationwide effort. Though the collaborative effort did not win the competition, the Horizon House represents innovation in planning, with the firm providing a two-story structure stacking at its center, each story reaching out with perpendicular wings into the landscape. Furthermore, the design incorporated vertically stacked horizontal concrete masonry units and poured-concrete slab construction. Large windows balance the heavy masonry feel of the building. Typical of Loewenstein interiors, the public rooms include a warm pallette of materials — paneling, a beamed ceiling, and mid-century Modern furnishings. Found underfoot throughout the first floor, concrete pavers remind the users of the structure that the designers employed concrete products at every turn. Gregory Ivy wrote to Knoll Associates to inquire whether the modern furniture concern would assist with furnishing the house.[9]

Horizontal concrete masonry units stacked one over the other, poured concrete panels with a pebbled surface, and standard concrete masonry units show some of the variety of concrete as required by Horizon House Competition entries. Large windows contrast the enclosed feeling of the structure. An open deck, surrounded by a pierced low wall, provides outdoor living space adjacent to the living room. The floor of the second-story deck caps the rooms on the first floor. Cantilevered bedrooms on the southwest and northeast sides of the structure, suspended over a lower deck and the main entrance of the house, suggest a dynamic quality at blending indoor-outdoor space. Working around the trees on the wooded lot, the Horizon House nestles into its hilly site. Changes in elevation make possible the variety of outdoor spaces at the periphery of the building. (LAA)

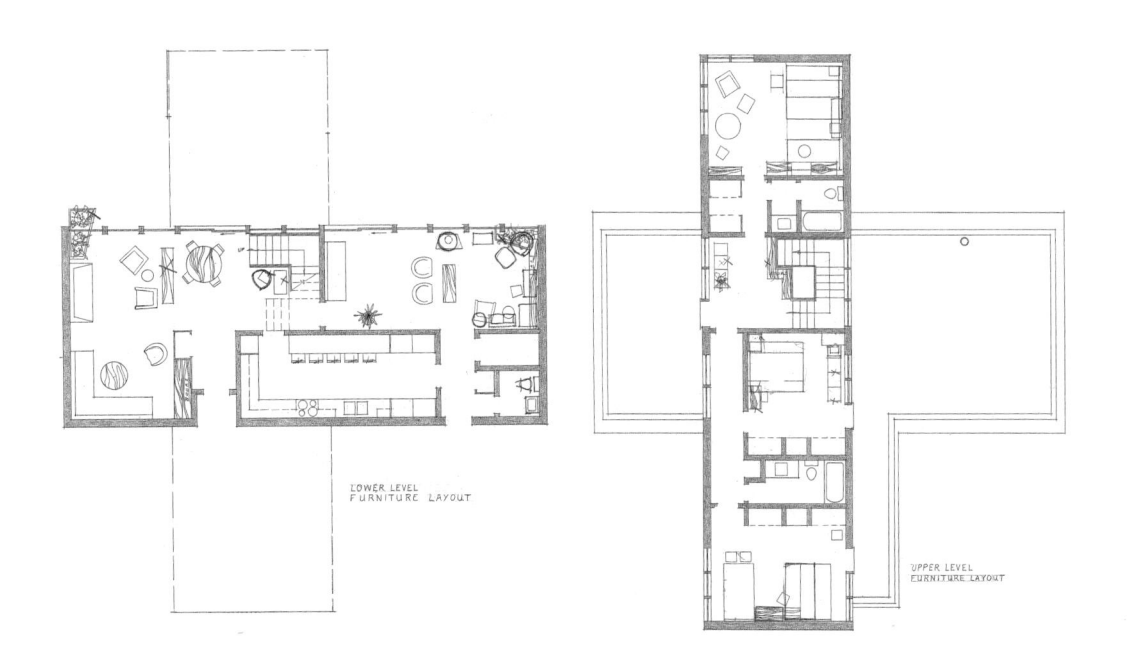

The second floor, containing three bedrooms and two baths, borrows techniques of compartmentalization in the private areas from many Loewenstein commissions. The encased stair hall provides access to one bedroom through its adjoining bath and a hallway that opens onto two bedrooms in the opposite direction. The enclosed kitchen includes all electric appliances, following the lead of similar configurations in the Commencement Houses and reflecting the surge in interest for homes powered solely by electricity. (LAA)

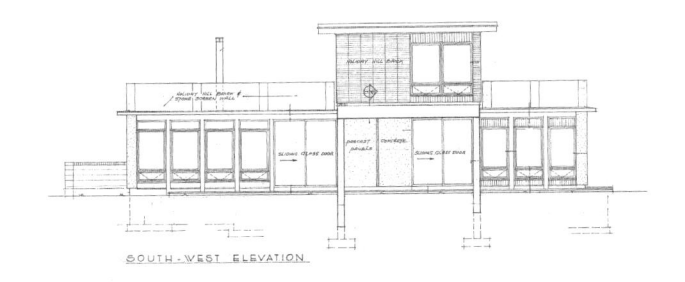

A galley kitchen and the staircase divide the first floor of the scheme into two living spaces. Dining takes place along a counter in the enclosed kitchen or at an open table near the staircase. Mid-century furnishings complement the simple interior of the stair hall and adjoining living space. Warm-hued paneling, concrete pavers on the floor, and a stippled concrete beamed ceiling bring together a variety of textures and finishes in the public spaces of the interior. (LAA)

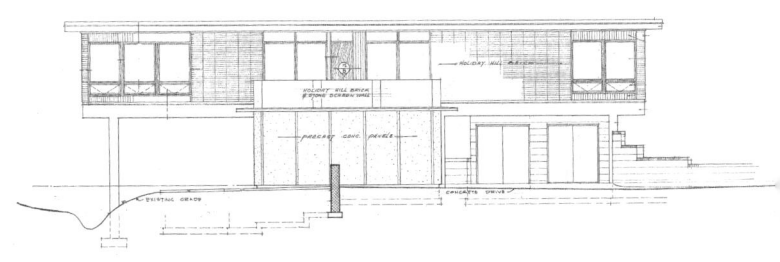

The neat geometry of the Horizon House is apparent in its elevations, where all building features and details conform to a four foot wide rhythm throughout the structure. The contrasting types of concrete provide interest and variety along the façade. (LAA)

LEAH + A. J. TANNENBAUM RESIDENCE : GREENSBORO (1963)

Dr. A. J. Tannenbaum, Greensboro physician, had retained Loewenstein-Atkinson for work on five renovations of his medical office (at 1001 N. Elm Street) over a period of two decades. And in 1961, he commissioned Loewenstein (his patient) to design a new home for him. The house, in supervision stage by 1962, certainly represents the largest residence the firm designed at the time. It predates the smaller Willis and Steele Residences, as well as a variety of other projects: two schools, a bank building, three factories, and bids for the public library. The design represents a departure from Loewenstein's customary layouts for houses of this size, in that he organizes the plan around a central court.

Documents from the firm's archive offer the rare opportunity to see the design process in action. Over a six-month period from 5 April to 15 September 1951, Loewenstein and employees of the firm penned seven plans showing iterations of the same basic ideas. As in his other large houses, Loewenstein used built-ins to divide public and private, both conceptually and physically. He organized the plan around a courtyard or light court containing small pool and fountain features with access on all four sides to breakfast room, family room, gallery, and hallway. Rather than spreading wings into the landscape, a more customary practice for Loewenstein designs, here the bedroom wing encloses the courtyard, an exterior space, within the scheme. Both living room and dining room lay at the entrance to the dwelling with an atrium space that through light knits the two together. Loewenstein experimented with curving walls (as he had done in both his own home and the Chandgie Residence). Furniture studies and interior elevations further demonstrate the care with which Loewenstein and his colleagues brought the design vision to fruition.

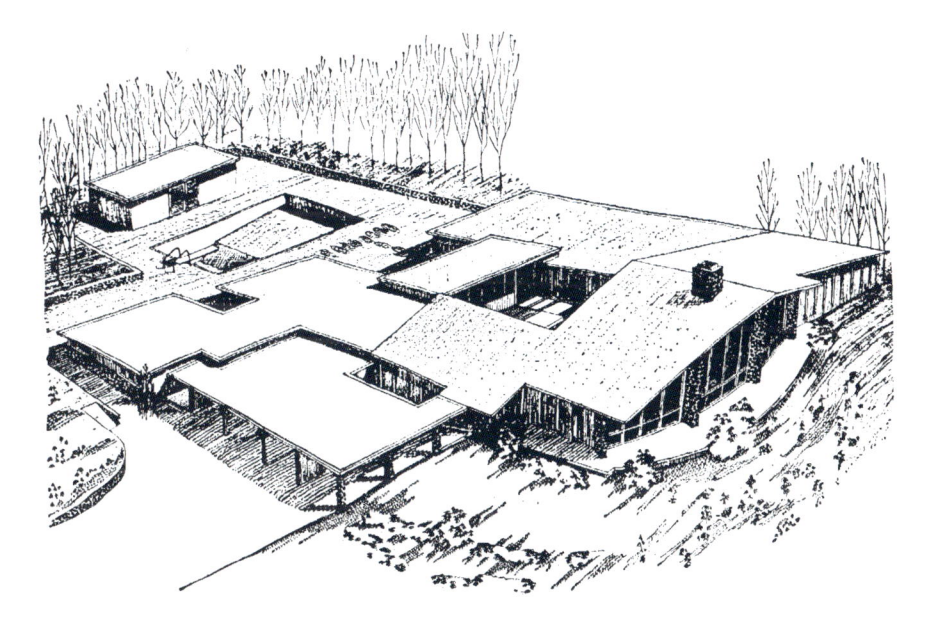

This axonometric drawing indicates not only the location of the organizing, central courtyard in the main block of the Tannenbaum Residence but also the relationship of the pool house to the main house, demonstrating how Loewenstein and members of the firm sought to capture views of the landscape for the residents. The design represents a departure from Loewenstein's customary layouts for houses of this size, in that he organizes the plan around the central court. (*Greensboro Daily News*, hereafter GDN)

The signature space, at the middle of the design scheme, echoes the atrium houses of the Mediterranean basin, including houses that Loewenstein saw on his visit to Pompeii in 1961. The layout for the Tannenbaum Residence follows earlier efforts at Carter, Loewenstein, and Davis commissions, but Loewenstein takes it a step further here in that the private wing of the house closes the view and captures exterior space within the confines of the structure. (GDN)

The visitor enters the structure to see an overscaled, copper fireplace hood and raised hearth (*left*). In front of the mass, a curved sofa helps define the living room space and the seating within it. Furnishings in the library (*center*) hint at the kind of eclecticism Sarah Hunter Kelly espoused. Gregory Ivy assisted with selections in furnishings throughout the interior. (GDN)

The low profile of the structure echoes Loewenstein's earlier houses. A four-bay carport confronts the visitor on the driveway; the front pedestrian entrance lies at the right side of the composition. (GDN)

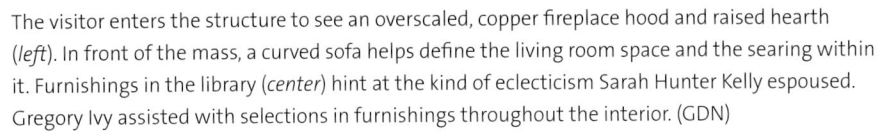

The firm maintained terrific documentation on the dwelling, from conception through design development and into supervision and inspection. The set includes 42 drawings, as well as a series of sheets affixed together at a scale of 1"=1'-0", which when unfolded measures approximately 20' x 20'. It is not clear why members of the firm made this large-scale representation. The drawings indicate that an RAS Jr. and RK both worked on the house design. The latter is Richard Kidd, who worked for the firm from at least the early 1950s through the late 1970s. It is unclear whose initials RAS Jr. represent, but they are recorded on two of the sheets in the drawing set. Outside of this tangible evidence, Clinton Gravely and Frank Harmon remember designing some small details in the house, including doorknobs and light fixtures.

Firm records indicate that Sedgefield Garden Center accomplished the landscaping for the property; the Sink Electric Co. completed the light scheme (not Thomas Smith Kelly) and Gregory Ivy coordinated interior design, in consultation with Sarah Hunter Kelly. Copies remain of several letters from the 1960s written by members of the firm with no return correspondence from Kelly, suggesting perhaps transactions by telephone or in-person visits. According to oral tradition, Kelly did visit the Tannenbaum Residence as it neared completion and an extant fabric samples collection indicates her involvement in the interiors of the home.

The Tannenbaum Residence appears on a list of properties and projects to be recorded through images for the firm, notably also including the **Greensboro Public Library** (1964). In 1965, Haycox Reprographic, Inc. photographed the structure to include in the *New Homes Guide*. The firm also saw the house published in *House + Garden Magazine* (1963) and in a one-page spread in the *Greensboro Daily News* (4 April 1964) because the house was the featured property on the Greensboro Council of Garden Clubs' House and Garden Tour in April 1964.

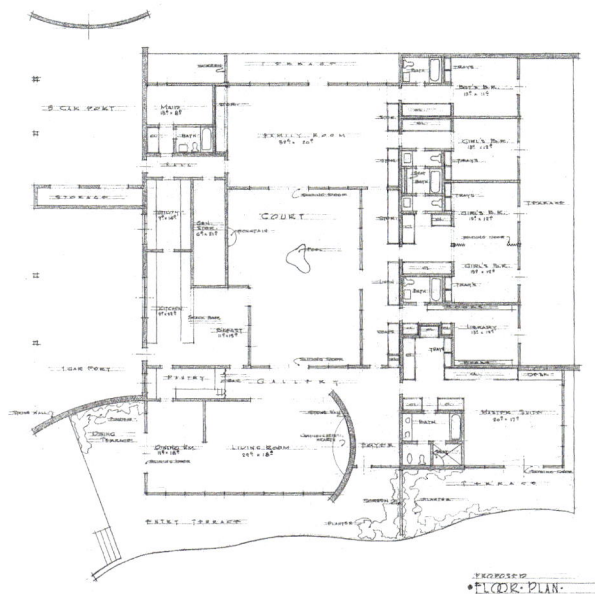

Plan B (*below*), 7 April 1961, keeps the basic same plan configuration but adds a passageway between carport and house and increases the size of the breakfast room. The plan also reconfigures the built-ins separating public and private spaces, eliminating storage on exterior of bedrooms, widening the circulation space and labeling it study, and eliminates storage on the long wall in master bedroom. (LAA)

Tannenbaum Residence, Plan A (*above*), 5 April 1961. (LAA)

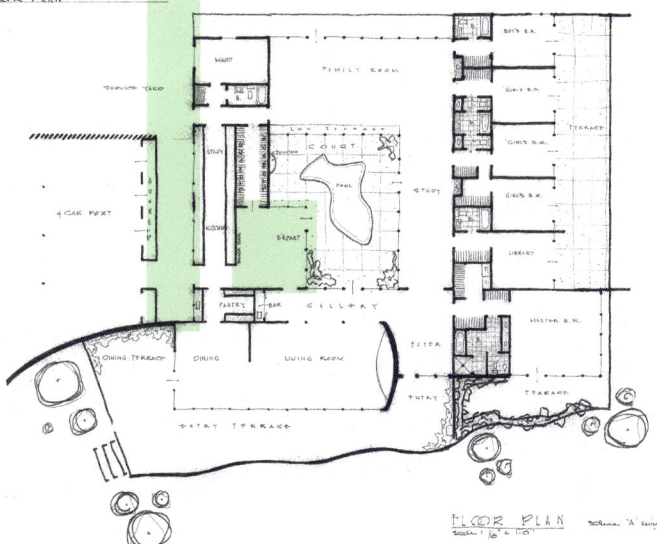

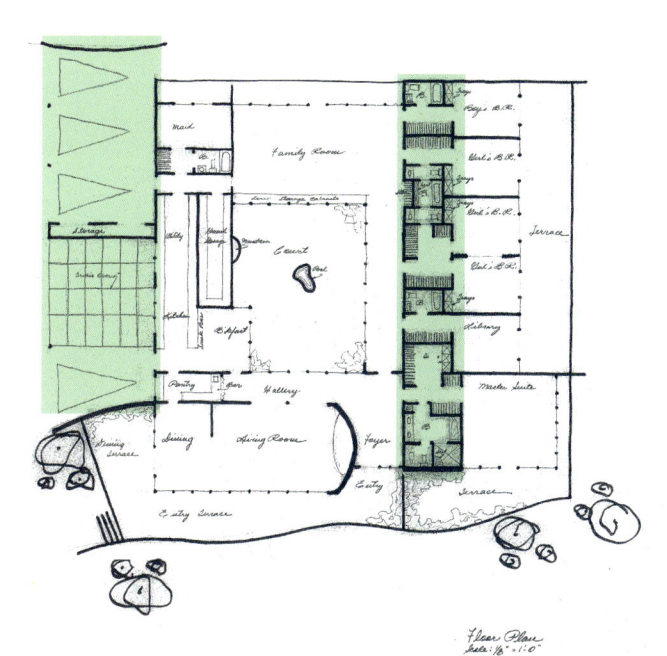

Plan C (*above*), 19 April 1961, retains the same basic plan configuration as before but closes one end of the pantry, reduces the size of the breakfast room, and continues to tweak built-ins. (LAA)

Plan D (*below*), 28 April 1961, breaks up the galley kitchen and storage scenario slightly and simplifies the court to a rectangle (rather than slight L). (LAA)

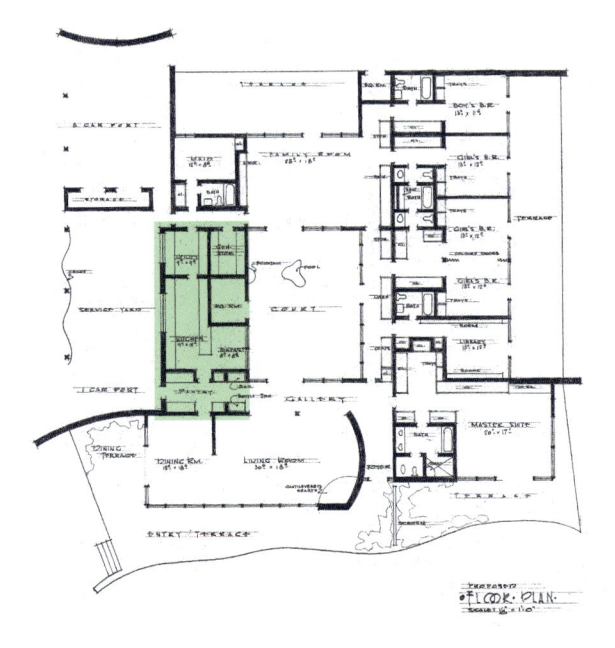

Plan E (*below*), 31 May 1961, significantly reorients the plan, renaming the family room a teenage room, renaming the living room a family room, and altering the configuration of the latter in relation to the dining room. The new plan also introduces a study as a separate room (no longer a wide hallway) and a new arrangement for master bedroom closet and bath. The boy's room is moved next to the maid's room; the kitchen is rearranged; and the carport entry/laundry drying area is shifted. (LAA)

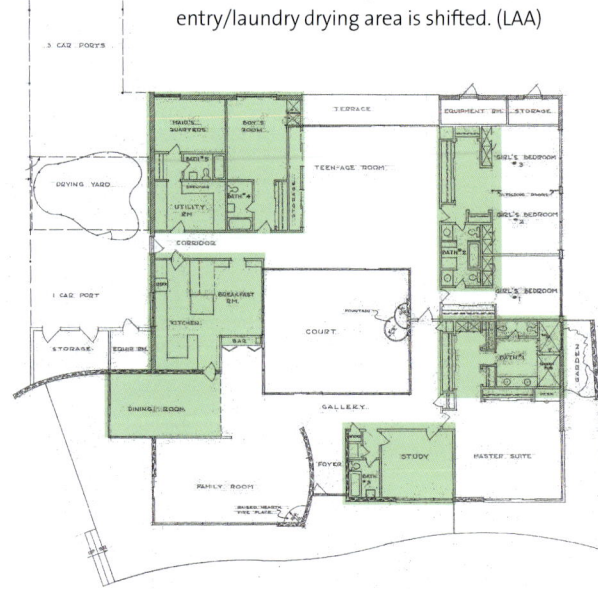

Plan F (*above*), 5 June 1961 (drawn by RK), is similar to Plan E but changes the size and shape of the dining room and the size and shape of rear terrace and end of bedroom suites. It also alters the size and location of the guest bathroom near the study and integrates the courtyard more fully. (LAA)

Plan G (*below*), 15 June 1961 (drawn by RAS Jr. and revised 5 and 7 July 1961), shows the design nearing its final configuration. Major changes include the addition of a curving wall along living room and study, reconfiguration of the entrance to carport side of building, an angled carport, a new pool and poolhouse, and minor alterations to the bedroom "wing" at the end of the pool. At this point in the process, the commission receives job number (325) signaling a shift from preliminary design to design development. (LAA)

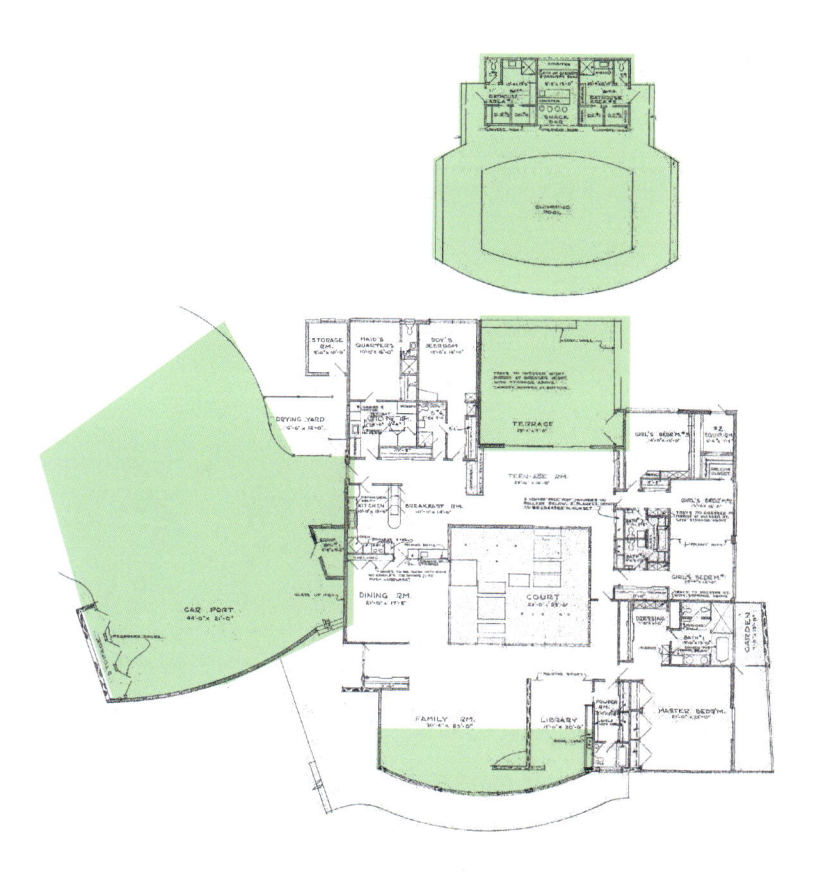

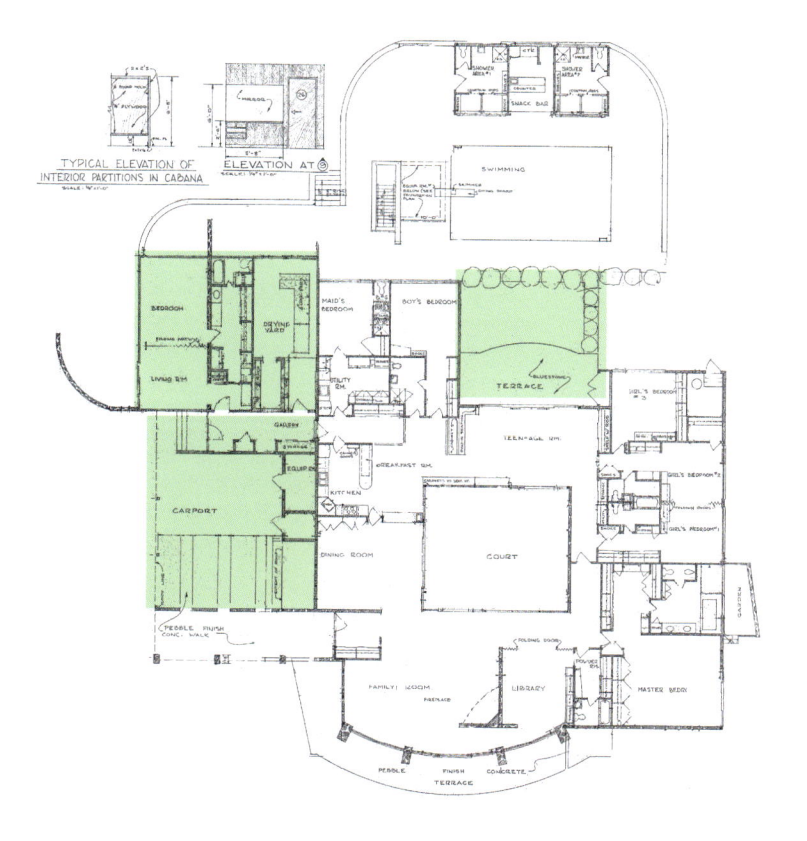

Plan H (*above*), 15 September 1961, removes the angled carport, adds a mother-in-law unit (living room, bedroom, dressing/bathroom), reconfigures the laundry work room (moving it from outside to inside), and incorporates a more elaborate service entrance (but now streamlined along the kitchen). The firm included the design for the patio areas around the pool and pool itself. (LAA)

JOAN + RICHARD STEELE RESIDENCE : GREENSBORO (1964)

At the Steele Residence, Loewenstein stacked up his more typical one-story buildings into a two-story scheme, nestling the structure into a hilly but compact 100' x 140' site. Clerestory, picture, and awning windows abounded on this structure, providing the interior with tremendous light. Neighbors noted how much time Loewenstein invested in ensuring that the structure was placed correctly, given the hilly site with water issues. Florence Snider tells of the time when she looked out her kitchen window, wondering who the tall man was wearing headphones, looking around the then vacant lot next door. Upon inquiring, she learned that Loewenstein was learning Italian by listening to recordings while he was speculating about the best fit for the house he envisioned on the property. As with many he met, Loewenstein became life-long friends with Mrs. Snider and her husband, Bill, an editor at the *Greensboro Daily News*.[10]

Loewenstein's design challenge for this structure came in the form of collected objects and artifacts from the extensive travels of the couple who hired him. Willing to accommodate these requests, Loewenstein demonstrated again his commitment to responsive client service. The Steeles concurred that Loewenstein accommodated their wishes in his design for their residence: "It was best to give him free reign in the initial design rather than hamper his drafting with practical concerns about budget and storage necessities. While keeping the initial flare, he was more likely to be able to alter his designs, making them less expensive and keeping budget in mind."[11] The structure that resulted bridged the old and the new, housing traditional elements and artifacts in a Modern architectural shell.

Top: Along the east side, the Steele Residence nestles into its wooded lot. Carefully manicured gardens and lawns contribute to the sense of outdoor rooms adjacent to the house. All of the rooms in the lower level are oriented to receive the filtered light from the east. (CTB)

Right: The Steeles salvaged an Edenton fireplace surround and, like the many treasures they collected from extensive world travels, asked that Loewenstein incorporate the artifacts into the mid-century structure, a task he accomplished handily. The living room features many storage cupboards and bookshelves designed to integrate the Edenton mantle into the interior scheme. Uplighting draws attention to the ceiling, uncharacteristic for Loewenstein in its austere finish. Pecky cypress siding, brick, and slate used throughout the interior tie the building to the landscape through materials. Wood paneling and grasscloth wallpaper complement this natural palette, while uplighting highlights all material surfaces. (CTB)

A glass shelved cabinet (*above left*), designed for the Steeles to display souvenirs from their world travels, sits between front hall and living room, serving as a screen of sorts. This built-in echoes those at the Bertling Residence. An accordion door (*above right*) divides living room from the dining room before and after the evening meal, further evidence of compartmentalization within the public spaces of the design. (PLL)

A wood and copper wall screens the carport area from the entranceway to the structure, distinguishing public from private areas. The strong horizontal of the sloping roof and the wide overhangs balance the vertical emphasis of the south and east façades. Typical of most Loewenstein houses, a circulation space divides public from private with built-in storage to help shape the space. Between the center entry and the companion service door, the designers specified specially designed built-in cabinets for milk and mail delivery and for storing golf clubs. (CTB)

Working drawings show the Edenton fireplace mantel and its impact on the aesthetics of the living room. The firm took a cue from the mantel to design panels throughout the space. (LAA)

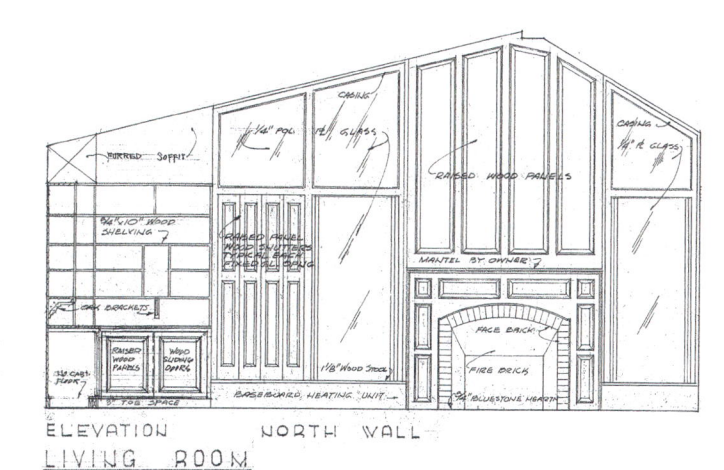

101

ANNE + JAMES H. WILLIS RESIDENCE : GREENSBORO (1965)

To prevent trees from being cut down for its construction, Loewenstein carefully inserted this simple structure into its site atop a steep hill. No formal landscape planning took place on the site, with the owners of the site preserving the woods they found there. Loewenstein organized this 3,100-square-foot house, around an L-shaped floor plan. The private wing separates from the main wing of the house by one step, making it a split-level design. A linoleum floor in the public wing balances the wall-to-wall carpet in the private wing. Built-in bookshelves surround the living room walls; a fireplace provides visual focus on one living room wall. Wide eaves protect the floor to ceiling windows on the north side of the house and provide an abundance of natural light as well as an uninhibited view of the landscape. Natural elements present throughout the house include slate flooring in the entryway, walnut paneling in the living room, and birch kitchen cabinets and panels.

Light sweeps through the north windows and sliding doors into the living and dining spaces. A beamed ceiling echoes the Loewenstein-designed structures of the 1950s. A fireplace, embedded in sets of shelves to the left and right, serves as the central focus for the east wall of the living/dining room. Its light-colored brick and position further underscore its symbolic importance. (CTB)

Above left: With a gable end facing the street, the front block of the Willis Residence contains living room, dining area, and kitchen, as well as a screened porch to the right. The public zone of the building protects the rear block of bedrooms from street view. (PLL)

A long hallway, the most characteristic feature of Loewenstein houses, connects all the bedrooms along one circulation path, linking public to private in the front hall. The designers rendered this hallway with simple materials and trim, consistent with Loewenstein's minimal aesthetic. (LAA)

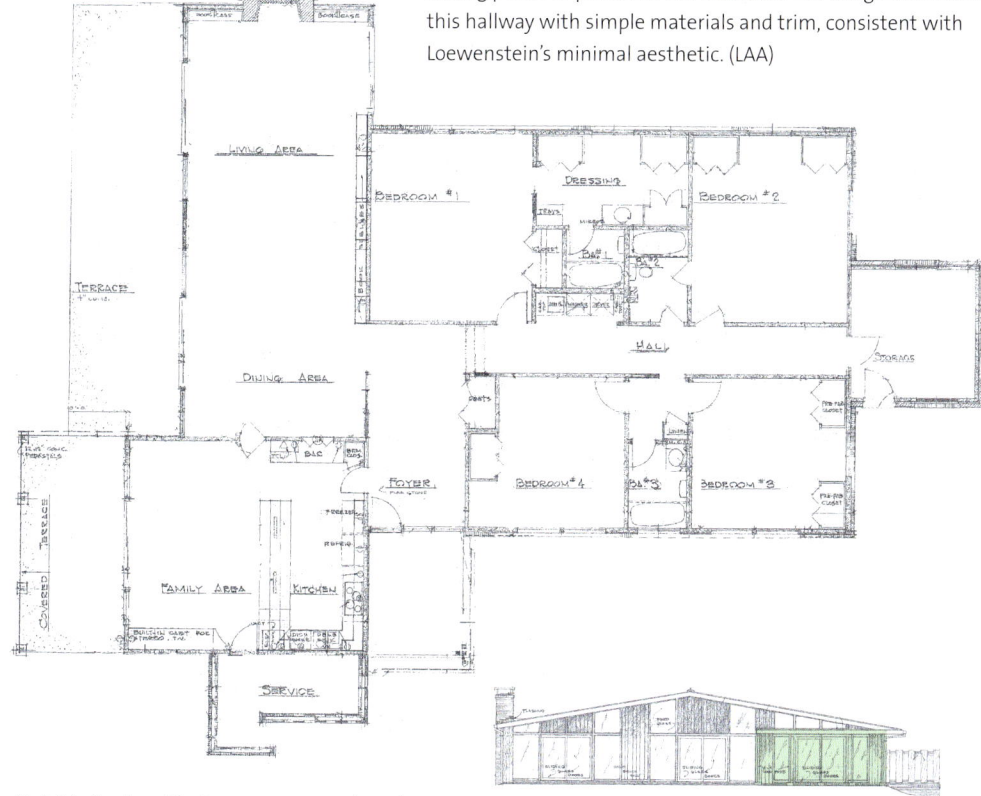

Outside the breakfast area, a screened porch (*top elevation on the right, to the right*) supplies a transitional zone between exterior and interior and draws occupants from the kitchen to the outdoors. The firm labels the street elevation (facing north) as the left side elevation and the west elevation, with its hidden front door, as the front of the structure. (LAA)

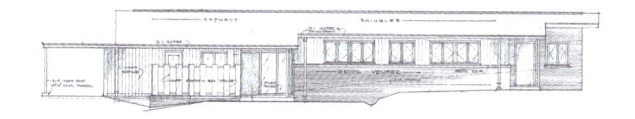

Random-pattern slate on the front hall floor contrasts with the linoleum tile in the public spaces and wall-to-wall carpet in the bedroom wing. This simpler stone represents a shift in level of interior finish from Loewenstein's earlier houses. (PLL)

Cabinetry defines three sides of the simple kitchen. A pass-through connects the kitchen with the adjoining breakfast room space. The double-sided cabinets contain ample storage for kitchen equipment, as well as diningware and accessories. The maple cabinets and paneling, in honeyed tones, add warmth to the rooms. Copper pulls, simple details lovingly restored by the house's current owners, continue to serve functionally and aesthetically. (PLL)

JOAN + HERBERT FALK RESIDENCE : GREENSBORO (1966)

This single story, side-gabled building contains a central chimney to divide public and private zones — living room, family room, screened porch, and kitchen to the south, and a four-bedroom block on the north. Within the decidedly horizontal brickwork, Loewenstein creates a pierced pattern on the brick rowlock surrounding the front garden, bringing this same detail to the pierced brick wall panels in the left garden. Covered on the back side with aluminum mesh, the square openings serve as garden drains on one side while continuing the front façade detail. Loewenstein employed an array of traditional and Modern window types on the structure. The asymmetrical front elevation, with its off-center door flanked by slender glass-pane sidelights, mirrors compositional work of previous houses but grounded itself with more typical elements that represent the common suburban idiom of Irving Park. The compact elevation spread less than earlier designs and thus revealed a hybrid structure, halfway between Modern and suburban vernacular forms. The similar, lively mix of interior appointments also characterized this house as a hybrid. Smaller in square footage and reflective of more conservative values, this hybrid house reflected tighter budgetary constraints and a smaller lot than Loewenstein's other houses. The Falks did not employ a live-in maid, removing the need for a separate "service" entrance or wing and a bedroom.

The south (*top*) and north (*bottom*) elevations of the Falk Residence suggest a building much more in keeping with contemporary suburban design, complete with low sloped roofs and stock windows. (LAA)

Loewenstein flipped the family room/screened porch to the rear of the structure (directly opposite its orientation at the Carter Residence and the majority of his other Modern dwellings), resulting in the family room sandwiched between living room and screened porch. A series of sliding panels deflect visitors from access to the bedroom hallway. (LAA)

Lush landscaping complements the Falk Residence, softening and tying the house to the land. Mature trees, preserved from a wooded lot, further soften the impact of the structure, in contrast to its neighbors. (PLL)

Decorative art glass, embedded in the three window lights of the front door, show collaborator Gregory Ivy's impact on the structure in the specification of Modern finishes. (PLL)

Ivy's handsome copper and glass light fixture glows at the apex of the entry hall wall, bringing visual interest and light to the space. Ivy also designed a coordinating light fixture in the dining room. (PLL)

notes

1. Loewenstein to Stern, 17 February 1966, Loewenstein-Atkinson archives (private collection, Greensboro, NC, hereafter LAA).

2. Loewenstein to Molitor, 29 January 1962, LAA.

3. Ivy to Molitor, 16 March 1962, LAA.

4. Loewenstein to Carpenter, 5 May 1965, LAA.

5. Jane Loewenstein Levy remembers traveling with her father and Libbie Cone to Pompeii, recalling her father's strong interest in the atrium dwellings of the ancient world. Jane Levy interview, 16 June 2010.

6. W. K. Menash to Loewenstein, 3 July 1961, LAA.

7. John Q. Blodgett, American Embassy in Ghana, to Loewenstein, 12 July 1961, LAA.

8. Loewenstein to William B. O'Neal, 23 December 1964, LAA.

9. Ivy to J. Carlyle Hammer, 11 July 1962, LAA.

10. Interview with Florence Snider, Greensboro, NC, March 2006.

11. Interview with Joan and Richard Steele, Greensboro, NC, October 2007.

Ann and Lloyd P. Tate Residence, Pinehurst (1952). This 8,000-square-foot building was one of only a few Loewenstein two-story schemes in his body of Modern work and included a screened porch, outside eating patio, and a narrow sun porch on the second floor to expand the indoors to the outdoors. The five-bedroom, eight-bathroom house incorporated a live-in maid's suite on the second floor. A stair, detailed with open risers and railings, connected the two levels at the center of the scheme. This building was demolished in the 1980s. (Private collection)

the legacy of modernism today

The architectural legacy of Edward Loewenstein, cut short by his untimely death in 1970 and inherited by two subsequent generations of residents, has experienced some significant losses. In Pinehurst, Loewenstein's Modern dwelling was demolished in the late 1980s. In the 1990s, two major houses in Greensboro were razed to make way for cul-de-sac developments on their large lots. Two additional houses in Greensboro were lost in the first decade of the twenty-first century, again because property owners valued the land more than the buildings themselves. Despite these losses, many have come to appreciate the timelessness and utility of the Loewenstein designs and continued caring for — in some cases meticulously rescuing and restoring — the two dozen buildings featured in this catalog.

Though these five losses represent one attitude that dismisses Modern dwellings, another positive attitude persists in the community about the utility and comfort of these homes and the important history they embody. Because the buildings are adaptable to change, both subtle and monumental, and because they are located in an interspersed manner with more traditional structures, Loewenstein's fully modern and hybrid houses provide a touchstone, a window to the past, that reminds us today of their importance in the history of our community.

Libbie and Clarence Cone Residence, Sunset Drive, Greensboro (1954). Loewenstein designed the spacious two-story residence for a large lot at the intersection of Nottingham Road and Sunset Drive. Uniting the scheme under deep eaves, the brick house contains both a two-story section to the west and a corresponding one-story section on the east. Loewenstein gathered windows into large and regular groupings along all façades, lending a contemporary air to the structure, somewhat still embedded in the more traditional language of the Irving Park neighborhood. Very little photographic documentation survives of the interior, though shop drawings from the Crane Company Display Rooms (Greensboro) indicate an elaborate series of built-in cases and storage units throughout the home. Developers demolished the structure in the mid-1990s with the lot divided for two larger houses. This family photograph is a rare view of the Modern structure. (Nancy Cone Hanley and Barbara Cone McPhail)

Martha and Ceasar Cone II Residence, Cornwallis Road, Greensboro (1955). In designing the Cone Residence, Edward Loewenstein placed the building on its site to take advantage of the orientation and views. One of a few two-story structures designed by the firm, the exterior of the building featured an asymmetrical façade with stained vertical board siding on the second floor over light-colored buff brick on the first floor and at the rear of the structure. The façade telescopes toward the street at the left of the scheme, while the long driveway and parking areas provide access to the covered walkway and the front door. A large picture window connected living room to street view at the right of a covered entrance; a one-story screened room stood further to the right of the main building mass. The designers called for retention of many of the trees on the lot during construction. The H. Chambers Company provided interior design services for the home. The structure, remembered by many as home to one of the most prominent families in town, was demolished in the mid-1990s and the land subdivided for a cul-de-sac development now occupied by Grey Oaks Circle. (Carol W. Martin/Greensboro Historical Museum Collection)

Juliet and Oscar Burnett Residence, Lafayette Drive, Greensboro (1954). Edward Loewenstein and Oscar Burnett enjoyed a warm professional relationship, Loewenstein providing many designs for Burnett's company, the Bessemer Improvement Corporation. When Burnett invited Loewenstein to design a residence for his family, the architect delivered a one-story structure, spreading into the landscape at the edge of its Greensboro County Club lot. While large windows opened onto the rear of the property, the L-shaped front entry remained relatively closed to the street. Hallmark features included low, wide eaves and warm brick walls, as well as clerestory windows and built-ins throughout The plan incorporated both a crafts and a recreation room for the two children of the household, these two rooms occupying the northeast end of the house with the public rooms at the center of the scheme. After preliminary design had been completed. Loewenstein asked New York designer Sarah Hunter Kelly to offer comments and criticisms on the layout; Thomas Smith Kelly provided the lighting plan for the structure, marking another instance of both designers affiliating with Loewenstein projects in Greensboro. Current property owners demolished this house in 2007.

Frances and Irvin Squires Residence — Commencement House #1 — North Elm Street, Greensboro (1958). A developer eyed the land under the first Commencement House, along with neighboring houses, to amalgamate properties near the corner of Cornwallis Road and Elm Street for a townhouse development. The house was demolished in 2010.

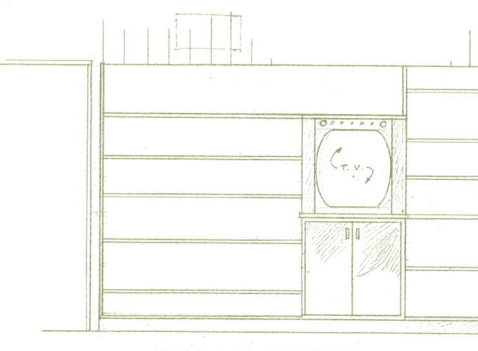

Students conceptualized a multi-sited exhibition and a series of events to advance knowledge about Modernism in Greensboro. With funding from the Cemala Foundation, the Marion Stedman Covington Foundation, the UNCG Department of Interior Architecture, the UNCG Office of Leadership and Service-Learning, and the UNCG Office of Undergraduate Research, the students joined their peers in art and history to produce the exhibit, including a web presence. Partners in the community included Preservation Greensboro, Inc. and Preservation North Carolina.

THE LOEWENSTEIN LEGACY

As an initiative of the Weatherspoon Art Museum, the Department of Interior Architecture at the University of North Carolina at Greensboro (UNCG) in 2005 organized a symposium and tour of homes to celebrate Loewenstein houses and their neighborhood contexts. Over the course of two days, property owners graciously shared their well-loved residences as more than 525 Modernism enthusiasts toured eight houses and an additional 380 people attended the symposium. Clearly, there was significant interest about the mid-century time period and the buildings that expressed something progressive about Greensboro. The symposium, events, and tour that made up "The Loewenstein Legacy" led to several additional activities and an entire research agenda at the University of North Carolina at Greensboro. The next year, community volunteers raised funds to establish a scholarship in Edward Loewenstein's name, in part to recognize his incredible contributions to design education at the university through his work with the Commencement Houses.

So great was the success of the symposium and tour that an exhibit on Modernism took form in the fall semester 2007, again centered in UNCG's Department of Interior Architecture but with significant support from the Department of Art, Department of History, Office of Undergraduate Research, and Office of Leadership and Service-Learning, as well as financial support from the Marion Stedman Covington Foundation and the Cemala Foundation. Loewenstein stood as the exhibit's focus as students explored the discourse of nonconformity that mid-century Modernism represented.

Encountering Loewenstein's designs as reflections of community aspirations and challenges, students examined buildings as conscious shapers of values and as containers for social discourse and action — but, importantly, apart from their sites and contexts. Designers faced the challenges of making this story come alive in two separate exhibit spaces, working within a large design team (18 students) augmented by a design review group and a team of project advisors. Because the network involved in producing the exhibit spread far and wide, both on and off the university campus, the exhibit served as a form of conversation itself, reaching out from university to community, in the interpretation offered by the students and importantly echoing Loewenstein's own town-gown roles of the 1950s and 1960s.

Two ideas offered by the students repeatedly arose during the schematic development for the exhibits. In absence of the actual architecture but in an attempt to classify it and to elicit an emotional reaction to it, students kept coming back to the horizontal as a direction of emphasis in Loewenstein's architecture — and in mid-century Modernist architecture generally. As expressed by a broad, sweeping gesture, this horizontal datum tied together all components of the exhibit. In addition, it helped provide a structural manifestation of the long legacy of Modernism to the Greensboro scene and linked the various sub-themes of the exhibit into

Left: Students connected with a variety of people during the development and design of the exhibit and collateral events and activities. During the design review process, Debbie Nestvogel (*left*) and Krista Nanton (*right*) explain the final model for the Gatewood Gallery installation of the exhibit to Jane Loewenstein Levy, the architect's daughter, and Clinton Gravely, AIA, an apprentice from the Loewenstein firm, now working as Clinton Gravely, Architect, AIA. (PLL)

Bottom left: The iar301-411 studio gathers after a visit to Well•Spring retirement Community after conducting oral history interviews with a dozen of Loewenstein's original clients, one of the more meaningful interchanges in the project among generations. Front row (*left to right*): Jax Harmon, Jennifer Tate, Ashley Boycher, Rebecca Colangelo, Ana Monge, Krista Nanton; middle row (*left to right*): Rachel Pound, Michelle Bottenus, Shannon Ryan, Debbie Nestvogel, Jenelle Davis, Erin Davis, McKenzie Gates; back row (*left to right*): Jane Levy, Edgar Cabrera, Leah Rowland, Matt Jones, Rachel Walker, Gwen McKinney. (PLL)

Bottom right: Matt Jones, Edgar Cabrera, Jax Harmon, and Jennifer Tate undertake the design process as they construct the final model after an extended design review process. (PLL)

(*Left to right*) Anna Monge, Krista Nanton, Matt Jones, Shannon Ryan, and Rachel Walker stand beneath a [mod]moment on the campus of Elon University. One of twelve kiosks installed in the community, the students believed that spreading the message of Modernism could happen outside the two main exhibit sites. (PLL)

Completely conceived and built by students, the team puts the final touches on the last of the panels in a long hallway in the Elon University School of Law (formerly the Greensboro Public Library of 1964, designed by Loewenstein). The panels remain as a permanent installation for use by the Law School. (PLL)

With other students working in the background, project director Patrick Lee Lucas discusses content with graduate student Gwen McKinney in the final installation stages of the exhibition. (Jennifer René Tate)

the overall expression of Modernism outside the style centers in the United States and abroad. The students' second recurring idea — a moment — began with a conceptual notion of a decentralized exhibit spread throughout the community. Just as a moment of understanding comes from the discussion of ideas in a variety of settings, the architectural moment explains something about Modernism in a textural as well as experiential way. Since this was a key concept for the development of the exhibit in the community, the students turned the idea inward on their own thinking for the exhibit, resulting in a **[mod]moment** as the core to the gallery space.

The exhibit took place at the Gatewood Gallery in the Gatewood Studio Arts Building on the campus of UNCG and in a long hallway at the Elon University School of Law Building (formerly the Greensboro Public Library [1964], designed by Loewenstein). In addition to the two major exhibition spaces, students designed a dozen **[mod]moments**, information kiosks placed throughout Greensboro at significant buildings and spaces to show the impact of Modernism in a community that valued the tried and true. These kiosks served as three-dimensional, experiential signs for the exhibit and spread the ideas generated by the students into the community. This deconstructed, multi-sited exhibit thus helped to ask questions about the social impact of artifacts both situated within and removed from the community, about how novice exhibit designers responded differently to the blank canvases of gallery spaces and highly contextual mini-sites, and about the strategies for curating urbanism and architecture in particular, sited installations. Students carried forward the assessment of Modernism through **[mod]haus**, a virtual exhibit following the same themes.

The exhibition, an unmitigated success with well over 2,000 people attending in one month at all locations — and many more visiting content online — provided an opportunity for greater awareness of Loewenstein's work. As a result, original homeowners, firm employees, and long-time Greensboro residents stepped forward with additional documentation. This exhibition led to a series of additional research projects and, with the support from the Graham Foundation for Advanced Studies in the Fine Arts, the development of a Loewenstein website (http://modernismathome.net). Under the guidance of Patrick Lee Lucas, Ashley Warriner Andrews, Mira Eng-Goetz, Vanessa Morehead, Leah Rowland, Denise Smith, and Jennifer René Tate undertook research projects that spun from the wealth of resources and ideas about Modernism in Greensboro.

The installation in the Gatewood Gallery borrowed on Loewenstein's vocabulary without exactly attempting to reproduce it. The result included sweeping and soaring aspects of visitor experience, all the while taking in interesting stories on Loewenstein and the firm. Students designed, budgeted, fabricated, and specified all elements within the exhibition. They also wrote and illustrated all of the panels displayed for visitors to learn about Modernism in Greensboro. (Jax Harmon)

At the Gatewood Building on UNCG's campus, four hundred people attended the opening reception, a beehive of activity including a wide variety of events during the opening week of the exhibition in November 2007. (Jennifer René Tate)

MODERNISM TODAY

One of the key ideas behind the first house tour and symposium was to highlight Loewenstein's beautifully designed Modern structures. In the ten years since the initiation of that project, countless hours of research, conversation, advocacy, and story telling have resulted in a greater awareness of the special character of these mid-century modern dwellings and their place in the Greensboro community. That work has been the brainchild of Dabney Sanders and Jane Loewenstein Levy. Standing right with them through the various strands of the Loewenstein Legacy, property owners shared their stories and welcomed others in as they tirelessly opened their houses, dug through files, and unearthed plans and memories of days gone by. Students from the UNCG Department of Interior Architecture and others, working on undergraduate research projects, independent study courses, and several related masters thesis topics contributed in important ways to the gathering and dissemination of information.

The Loewenstein network is a special one, to be sure, and it continues to grow as people come to marvel at the remarkable history of this North Carolina community and the amazing architectural legacy left to us by Edward Loewenstein. As properties change hands, new owners appreciate anew the thoughtful and thorough efforts of many who helped to make these houses both graceful to the eye and effortless for their dwellers. In the end, Loewenstein's houses represent an important epoch in Greensboro's history, a time when many participated in a conversation about difference and fitting in. The gentle man whom we have all come to know — Edward Loewenstein — reminds us that well-grounded human relationships provide avenues for understanding and tolerance. Though his architecture, Loewenstein taught, and continues to teach, important lessons about how we dwell at home, even in a house some would call Modern.

The iar301-411 Fall 2007 exhibit design studio students gather on the steps of the 1965 Commencement House, bringing the project full circle As an initiative of Edward Loewenstein and 23 students from the University of North Carolina at Greensboro, the house was completed in Sedgefield. Forty-two years later, UNCG students studied the structure as part of Loewenstein's mid-century residential legacy. (PLL)

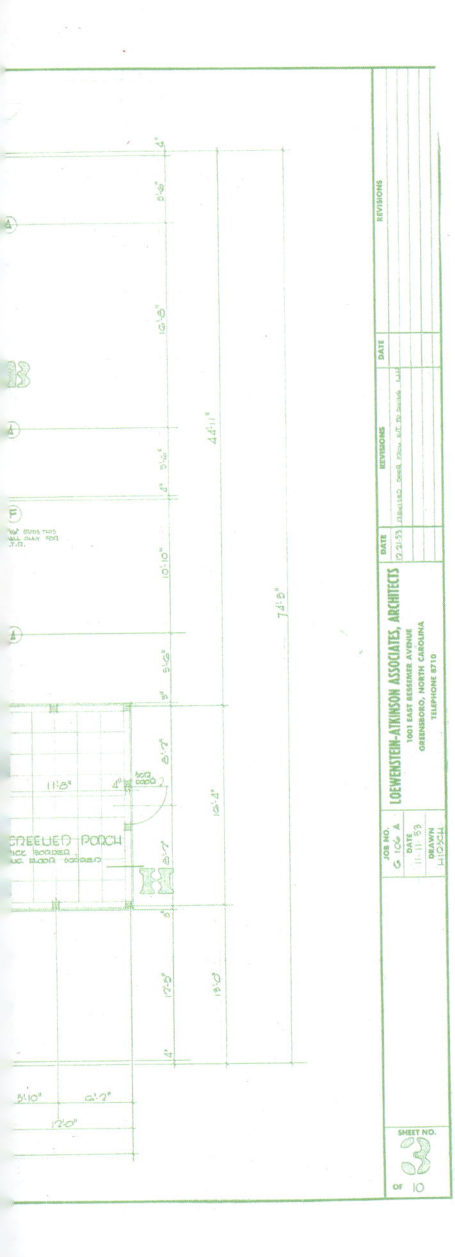

Photography and artwork:
C. Timothy Barkley Photography (CTB)
Bride's Magazine
Danny Fafard
Greensboro Daily News (GDN)
Jax Harmon
Loewenstein-Atkinson archive (LAA)
Patrick Lee Lucas (PLL)
McCall's
New York Times Magazine
Southern Architect (SA)
Jennifer René Tate
UNCG Special Collections and Archives (UNCG-SCA)
David Wilson/*UNCG Magazine*
Several private collections

Design: Donna Wojek-Gibbs

Set in: TheSans and ITC Stone Serif

Printed and bound by: GeoGraphics, Atlanta, GA

Printed on: Hanoart Silk